Joan 'n' The Whale

John Duckworth

Joan 'n' The Whale

L·I·F·E·S·C·A·P·E·S

Fleming H. Revell Company
Old Tappan, New Jersey

"Joan 'n' the Whale" reprinted from *FreeWay*, copyright 1978, Scripture Press Publications, Inc., Wheaton, Illinois 60187.

"The Christian Airplane" reprinted from *Sunday Digest*, copyright 1981 by David C. Cook Publishing Co., Elgin, Illinois 60120.

Unless otherwise identified, Scripture quotations are from the HOLY BIBLE: NEW INTERNATIONAL VERSION. Copyright © 1973, 1978, by the International Bible Society. Used by permission of Zondervan Bible Publishers.

Illustrated by Dan Pegoda.

Library of Congress Cataloging-in-Publication Data

Duckworth, John (John L.)
    Joan 'n' the whale and other stories you never heard in Sunday school.

    1. Christian fiction, American.   I. Title.
PS3554.U277J6   1987   813'.54   86-31318
ISBN 0-8007-1519-5

Copyright © 1987 by John Duckworth
Published by the Fleming H. Revell Company
Old Tappan, New Jersey 07675
Printed in the United States of America

TO Lizabeth—
who knows how
to take fun
seriously

Contents

Contents

The Parable
of the Preface 🖋

Once upon a time there was a girl named Goldilocks. She wanted some spiritual food, so she went into a bookstore. The first book she picked up was very heavy. It was called *An Extremely Long Treatise on Being Tremendously Spiritual, Including Lots of Stuff About Archaeology and Some Charts in the Back*. She tasted it.

"Too dry," she said.

So she picked up another book. It weighed almost nothing. Its title was *The Christian Celebrity Coloring Book of Favorite Recipes With Pictures of Baby Animals and Things*. She tasted it. It went down smoothly enough, but left her feeling as though she'd eaten nothing at all.

"Too frothy," she mourned.

Then she sighed. "If only I could find a book that was not too dry, not too frothy," she exclaimed. "One that was fun to read, but gave me something important to think about."

She was just about to leave the store when a third book caught her eye. It was not quite like any other book she had seen. Instead of being heavy, it was full of parables about mad scientists, Volkswagens, baseball players, and vacuum cleaners. Yet it was not too frothy, because each story had a point. It made her think about important things—in a different way.

She tasted it. "Ah," she cried. "Just right."
So she bought the book, brought it home, and ate it.
If you just want to *read* it, though, that's okay with me.

JOHN DUCKWORTH

The Parable of the Preface

Acknowledgments

Many of the stories in this book were first published in magazines and other periodicals. I'm grateful to the editors of those publications for first letting those stories see the light of day. Thanks to these publishers, especially to *Free-Way* for permission to reprint "Joan 'n' the Whale" and *Sunday Digest* for permission to reprint "The Christian Airplane"—and to the editors at the Fleming H. Revell Company.

Joan 'n' The Whale

1

Christianstein

It was . . . well . . . a dark and stormy night.

Thunder echoed from mountain to marsh as sheets of rain descended on the sleepy village of Saint Horribleburg. A flock of bats flapped into the gloom; the red eyes of unknown creatures glowed in the darkness. But the most frightening sight of all stood miles past the burghermeister's cottage at the edge of town, high on the brink of a forbidding cliff.

It was a castle—a castle whose cold, gray stones flashed white with each explosion of lightning. It was . . . the Castle Van Gelical!

Somewhere a wolf—or something—howled. Chains rattled, trees shivered, and even the wind seemed to moan over what was about to happen.

Inside the castle dungeon, an eerie light began to glow. A long, bony hand adjusted the flame of an oil lamp. The glow increased, dimly revealing a profusion of bottles, flasks, test tubes, and retorts that bubbled foul liquids over Bunsen burners. An odor of madness seemed to hang in the air, because this—this was the laboratory of the maddest scientist of them all. This was the laboratory of the infamous *Dr. Emil Van Gelical!*

A rat scrabbled across the granite floor as a gaunt figure stepped into the light. It was Dr. Van Gelical himself, wearing a once white laboratory coat now stained with the evidence of his notorious experiments. His cheek twitched; his wide eyes gleamed as he gazed at the sheet-covered table in the center of the room.

Under the sheet lay a human form. Or *was* it human? The crazed surgeon seemed to contemplate that question as he approached the table, rubbing his hands together, his mouth awry with a twisted grin.

Suddenly he turned toward the door. "Igor!" he shouted. "Come quickly. There is much work to be done!"

Irregular footsteps descended the dungeon staircase. In moments a shuffling, hunchbacked ragbag of an assistant appeared, carrying a candelabrum and a large cardboard box.

"Yes, master," Igor replied, groveling. "Here are the materials you ordered. All is in readiness!"

"Good, good," the doctor breathed. "Bring the materials to the table, Igor. It is time to begin . . . the experiment!"

The crash of a thunderbolt was heard as Igor dragged his box to the side of the table. "I *love* experiments, master," he said, fawning. "Even though the villagers say you are crazy—"

The doctor whirled. "Crazy, am I?" he bellowed, his cheek twitching furiously. "I'll show them who's crazy. Those fools in the village, calling me mad—how dare they? I'll show them—I'll show them all! I'll—"

"Of *course* you will, master," Igor soothed, bowing deeply. "Everyone knows you are a genius. The name of *Van Gelical* is known throughout the district, throughout the province—"

"And soon throughout the world!" the doctor declared.

"Yes, master," said Igor. "Perhaps your fame would have spread sooner if you hadn't borrowed the burghermeister's cerebellum before he was finished with it—"

"Silence!" shouted the doctor, glowering at his assistant. "That was a trivial matter, Igor, and one soon to be forgot-

ten. For tonight I will conduct the greatest experiment of my career. Tonight will be . . . my ultimate triumph!"

"Ooooh," Igor murmured. "I *love* triumphs!"

The doctor raised his fist heavenward. "I am going to achieve what no man has done before," he announced. "Tonight I create . . . spiritual *life!*"

Barooom, roared the thunder. Igor cringed. Flashes of lightning illumined the doctor's wild and slightly crossed eyes. "This is my finest hour, Igor," he cried over the din of the storm. "For tonight I create . . . *Christianstein!*"

A deafening thunderclap rocked the dungeon. Igor swallowed. "C-C-Christianstein?" he repeated.

"Yes, Igor," the doctor hissed, grasping his assistant's misshapen shoulders. "They call me a madman, an evil genius, a tamperer with nature. But tonight I will prove them wrong. Christianstein will be the greatest specimen of spiritual life the world has ever known! He'll have everything, Igor. Everything!"

Igor nodded vigorously. The doctor drew back. "Very well, Igor," he said. "Let the operation begin!"

"I *love* operations," Igor said, positioning himself at his master's side. He gasped as the doctor pulled the sheet from the table, uncovering the inanimate form of a young man who was dressed in a white shirt, gray tie, and blue polyester suit.

"The moment has come," the doctor intoned. "Give me my surgical gloves."

"Yes, master," Igor said and complied.

"Scalpel," came the next command. Again the assistant did as he was told. In rapid succession the forceps, sponges, clamps, and tubes followed. At length the perspiring doctor took a deep breath and consulted a clipboard; it was time to equip his creation.

"Give me the voice of a great evangelist, Igor!" he ordered.

"Yes, master," Igor replied and handed him a jar from the box.

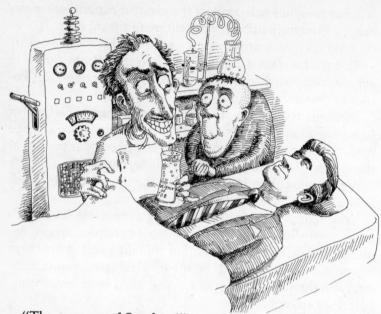

"The courage of Stephen!" came the next instruction. Igor produced a dusty vial.

"The patience of Job!" the doctor commanded and was rewarded with an ancient-looking flask.

After what seemed like hours, the doctor straightened from his labors. "Now, the hypodermic," he ordered, "and the serums I distilled."

Igor's hands trembled as he presented a long, steel syringe. From the box he brought a tray of bottles filled with weirdly colored fluids.

"Double doses of daily prayer and Bible reading," the surgeon murmured, withdrawing liquid from one of the bottles and injecting it into the lifeless figure's arm. "Then faithful church attendance . . . generous giving . . . temperance . . . volunteer work . . . ability to resist temptation . . . witnessing. . . ." He paused, then filled the syringe with fluid from the final container. "And last—but not least—a triple injection of . . . *orthodoxy!*"

18   Joan 'n' the Whale

Thunder boomed again as the doctor reread his clipboard list. "Examine the box, Igor," he said. "Have we forgotten anything?"

"Oh, no, master," his assistant answered, turning the carton upside down and shaking it. "Everything must be in place!"

"Excellent!" the doctor cried, yanking off his rubber gloves and fastening a pair of power cables to his creation's neck. "This is the moment the world has waited for. This is the moment for . . . Christianstein!"

He dashed to the nearest wall, where an electrical control panel waited. "A million volts of lightning will bring my creation to life," he declared. "Now stand back, while I throw the power switch . . . and prepare to meet the perfect Christian—*Christianstein!*"

Igor covered his eyes with his hands. With a flourish the doctor threw the massive switch from OFF to ON as an avalanche of thunder shook the castle. Lightning burst around them like a thousand suns; showers of sparks cascaded from the control panel as raw energy surged through the wires.

Smoke began to rise from the form on the table. Igor coughed, waving the fumes away. When they cleared, he beheld a heart-stopping sight.

The figure was quivering.

"Doctor!" Igor shouted. "He—he's moving!"

The surgeon rushed to see the figure raise its hand. "Yes, Igor, yes!" he cried. "My creation is—alive!"

Master and servant watched breathlessly as the thing called Christianstein slowly pulled itself to a sitting position. Then, stiffly, it climbed from the table and stood to its full height.

"Oooh," Igor breathed. "You've done it, master! He's perfect—the perfect Christian!"

"Oh, my creation," the doctor said, transfixed. "Speak to me!"

The figure looked down at the doctor and frowned. At last it began to speak—in a low and hostile growl:

"If I speak in the tongues of men and of angels, but have not love. . . ."

"Love?" said the doctor, scanning his clipboard with puzzlement.

Slowly the creature raised its arms in the direction of the doctor, who continued to consult his list. "If I have the gift of prophecy," it growled, "and can fathom all mysteries and all knowledge, and if I have a faith that can move mountains, but have not love. . . ."

"Love?" the doctor said impatiently. "Igor, what is he talking about?"

"I—I don't know, master," Igor answered, dropping to his knees and hiding under the table.

"If I give all I possess to the poor," the creature said, his voice building to a roar, "and surrender my body to the flames, but have not love. . . ." Suddenly he grabbed the doctor's laboratory coat and lifted him off the floor. "I . . . gain . . . *nothing!"*

The doctor gulped. "N-nothing?" he repeated. "N-not even a little something?"

"Aaarrggghhh!" the creature bellowed, dropping the doctor and reaching for his throat.

"Igor, you fool!" the doctor shouted, stumbling backward and scrambling for the door. "I knew we'd left *something* out!" He clambered up the stairs as his creation lumbered after him. "Such a little thing," the doctor cried, his voice fading into the distance.

Several minutes passed before Igor could find the courage to move. Slowly he looked out from under the table—first one way, then the other. Finally he spoke.

"I—I think we've created a monster," he whispered.

Somewhere a wolf—or something—howled.

2 The Beetle With the Rolls-Royce Nose 🌿

Far away, in a land where cars are more than mere steel and transmission fluid, there lived a Beetle. He was a 1967 Volkswagen Beetle, a little black one with dust and dents on his hood and gnats on his windshield. Underneath he was rusting, and his tires were balding; on top the sun had baked all the gloss out of his paint.

And of all the cars in the land, Beetle was surely the most miserable.

"What a homely thing I am," he would say with a honk, limping up and down the streets, out of tune. "And for all my mileage, where am I going? I'm not getting anywhere—just driving around in circles."

He had tried the standard remedies for depression. "Surely *this* will do it," he would say, filling his gas tank or changing his spark plugs or getting a new air filter. He had tried a custom-made muffler, a valve job, a new stereo system, a handwoven litter bag, and even an air freshener shaped like a pine tree.

But none of them worked. Deep down he was still the same old Beetle.

So he listened to the advice of other vehicles. "Try this high octane gas, pal," a shady-looking convertible told him. "Try gasohol," said a pickup truck. "Forget that stuff," said a sports car with a glazed look on its windshield. "What you need is a sniff of ether in your carburetor every morning!"

He tried them all, but it was no use. *I'm just an ugly old Beetle,* he cried to himself, *and that's all I'll ever be.*

One day, though, Beetle was droning dejectedly down the highway when he saw something that nearly made him cross the yellow line. It was a glistening, purring Rolls-Royce Silver Cloud, all dazzling chrome and wire wheels. Beetle watched wistfully as the automobile glided past. "If only I were a Rolls-Royce instead of a Beetle," he murmured, "then I'd be happy. Everyone would look up to me, because I'd have style and class."

He continued to gaze at the Rolls, admiration in his headlights, when all at once it came to him. He *could* be classy, just like a Rolls-Royce. He *could* have style!

Excited, he added up some figures on his odometer. Yes, it *was* possible! He had just enough money left in his glove compartment. Sputtering into high gear, he headed for the nearest Rolls-Royce dealership.

So the transformation began.

"Ow!" Beetle cried when they made the incision in his hood.

"Ow!" he said again when the bill was presented two days later.

It took every penny Beetle had. But when he emerged from the body shop, he was sure the ordeal had been worth it.

There he was, the proud possessor of a brand-new, gleaming Rolls-Royce nose. He stared at his reflection in a storefront window, mesmerized by the stately, sparkling grille with its prestigious double-R insignia and graceful ornament. It covered his old Beetle nose perfectly!

"I—I'm a new car!" he cried, and tootled toward the highway to show the other vehicles. Wouldn't *they* be impressed!

But they weren't. "Ha-ha!" laughed a Toyota. "Beetle got a nose job!"

"Good grief," said a BMW. "What incredibly bad taste."

Joan 'n' the Whale

"Ugh," said the Rolls-Royce Silver Cloud. "Give up, you low-class clattertrap. You're not a Rolls now, and you never will be."

Humiliated, Beetle blushed so hard that his engine began to overheat. He chugged off the highway and sat listening to the others laughing as they whizzed past.

A tear trickled down his bumper. Nothing would ever change, he knew now. Deep inside, he was still a homely old Beetle, driving around in circles. He could feel his battery beginning to wear down; maybe this time he wouldn't bother to recharge it.

He was just about to head for the wrecking yard when he noticed another car next to him. It, too, had pulled off the highway.

"What's wrong, Beetle?" the other car asked.

Beetle turned to behold the homeliest Studebaker he had ever seen—one so unstylish and unshiny that Beetle looked grand by comparison. But strangest of all, the old car looked *happy*.

"I—I don't understand," Beetle said. "How come you seem so happy? You're in worse shape than I am, but you look as if you know the secret of transportation. You even seem to know where you're *going*."

"I do," the Studebaker said, a smile playing around his headlights. "That's because I've got a purpose. I got it from the mechanic."

"The mechanic?" Beetle asked, then sighed."Too bad that wouldn't work for me. I've been to garages before. Nothing helps."

"You'll understand when you meet the mechanic," the other car said. "He's about three miles south, then turn right."

The Studebaker smiled again and was off. Beetle watched as the old car buzzed down the road. *It'll never work*, Beetle thought, turning south. *I'll just stop by on my way to the junkyard.*

When Beetle drove up to the big garage, the mechanic was waiting. "I've been expecting you, Beetle," he said warmly, wiping his hands with a rag.

"I met this Studebaker—," Beetle began.

"I know," the mechanic said with a smile.

Beetle looked the garage over. Cars of all kinds were there, some humbler than the Studebaker, some classier than the Rolls-Royce. Some were being repaired, but most seemed to be going places for the mechanic.

Beetle looked into the mechanic's gentle eyes and asked, "Can—can you fix me up?"

The man nodded. "You know I can, Beetle," he said.

Beetle felt his motor race. The Studebaker had been right. There *was* something different about this mechanic. He seemed to see right through Beetle's engine cover and to care what was inside.

"How—how much will it cost?" Beetle asked nervously.

"Everything," said the mechanic.

Beetle gulped. "But I don't have any more money," he said. "I spent it all on my Rolls-Royce nose."

The man smiled. "It's already paid for, Beetle. All you have to do is sign over your title and registration to me."

Beetle's hood nearly popped open. *"What?"* he beeped. "You mean you want to *own* me?"

"It's the only way," the mechanic said simply.

Beetle thought hard. Why, this was like being *totaled.* If he went through with it, there would be no turning back. He looked at the mechanic. He looked at the other cars, all dressed up and with places to go. Then he knew what he had to do.

Right there, he put himself in the care of the mechanic. He surrendered his title and registration. Within minutes his nose had been restored to its original condition—and he felt more excited than he had since the day he'd rolled off the assembly line.

"But I don't understand," he told the mechanic later as he

prepared for his first assignment. "I'm still just a homely, old, black 1967 Beetle. How come I feel so different?"

The mechanic chuckled. "Because," he said softly, "now you're *my* homely, old, black 1967 Beetle."

"Ah," said Beetle. So *that* was the secret of transportation. He headed for the highway, smiling from headlight to headlight.

3

I Don't Read
the Cookbook Anymore 🍃

I hardly ever read the Cookbook anymore.

Sure, some people say you should read it all the time, especially when you're going to *cook* something. But that sort of thing just isn't for me.

When I first became a chef, of course, I read the Cookbook all the time. In fact, *before* I was a chef, it was the Cookbook that showed me how to become one. I'd sit and read it for hours on end, poring over all those recipes, wishing I could bake and fry and whip up all those delicious-sounding dishes.

Then I got to the part of the Cookbook that tells you how to become a chef, and I went right ahead and followed directions. It was probably the happiest day of my life, come to think of it.

During those first months I almost always had the Cookbook under my arm wherever I went. People would ask me what that book was and why I was always carrying it around, and I'd practically glow as I told them all about how I'd just become a chef. I was so happy, I wanted everyone else to become a chef, too.

After two or three years, though, my study of the Cookbook began to fall off. After all, I figured, I was getting pretty good at this chef stuff now. I'd made most everything, from beef Stroganoff to petits fours, and they hadn't turned out too badly. Once in a while I'd accidentally skip an ingredient or use a pastry whip incorrectly, and the dish would flop. But I was getting quite a reputation as a cook and decided I didn't need to read the Cookbook so much.

Already I'd stopped carrying the unwieldy thing around with me, and now I stopped reading a portion of the general cooking instructions each day. So much of it was boring—especially the first two-thirds, which told the history of cooking and how they used to do things in the old days. *Who needs that?* I asked myself. *This is now. We've got microwaves and food processors—not brick ovens.*

Besides, I was just too busy for that stuff. To be a good chef, surely it would be enough just to cook. I didn't have to read and reread the Cookbook, too.

Next I started to cook without reading the recipes first. I'd already read most of the really popular ones, like pizza and scrambled eggs, at least once. Why bother to read them again? So I'd whip up a chocolate cake without peeking at the book, and to my surprise and pleasure it would turn out okay. True, sometimes I'd leave out the baking powder or use too much flour, but most of the time it was at least edible.

Before long I was making more complicated recipes without the book—things like soufflés and turkey tetrazzini. In some cases I'd never read the recipes at all, but I'd heard a lecture on the subject somewhere. Sometimes I hadn't even heard a lecture, but figured I knew enough about cooking to wing it.

I'd substitute ingredients and guess at baking temperatures, and sometimes the results weren't exactly the sort of thing you'd enter in the state fair. Once I came up with chocolate chip cookies you could drink through a straw—but they didn't taste too awful, I guess.

Eventually I couldn't remember many recipes, so I began to invent my own. I thought they were pretty close to the originals, but couldn't be sure since I'd misplaced my

Cookbook. Some people didn't think much of the dishes I invented—licorice burritos, for instance—but I didn't care. What was I supposed to do, anyway—memorize recipes?

A few of my cooking friends criticized me, saying I ought to read the Cookbook more. I tried to calm them down by buying a brand-new copy, a big one edged in gold. I brought it to cooking-society meetings, making sure everyone saw it. But I didn't open it, of course.

I *did* read cooking-*related* books—stuff about stoves and diets and grocery shopping. Some of those were quite interesting—and had pictures, which was more than I could say for the Cookbook itself.

Gradually, as my friends pestered me to get back into my Cookbook, I attended cooking-society meetings less and less. When a friend would express concern about my interest in cooking, I'd tell him I was watching one of those TV cooking shows regularly. And I was—for a while.

But my interest in cooking waned. Finally I stopped hanging around the kitchen altogether.

These days I don't do much cooking. If I get really hungry, I warm up a TV dinner. Once in a great while I'll get into a bind and have to whip up a hamburger, but the old zeal just isn't there anymore.

My old cooking friends just shake their heads now when they see me on the street. They look at each other as if to say, *Man, I'll bet he can't even remember how to boil water.*

What a bunch of know-it-alls. Of *course* I can remember how to boil water.

I just can't remember *why*.

4

Joan 'n' the Whale

Joan was in her dorm room, eating an Oh Henry bar, listening to the radio, and having her Quiet Time, all at once, when the Lord spoke to her. Out of respect she stopped chewing and turned the radio down a little.

"Joan," said God, "I want you to arise and go across the hall to Min Niniver, the girl who lives in room 207. And I want you to be her friend."

Joan giggled. Then she laughed so hard that her fish-shaped earrings and her cross necklace shook. "C'mon, God," she said. "Don't kid me. I'm a busy person. You know perfectly well I've got to study hard so I can go and be a missionary for you over in Upper Tarshishstan." She chuckled again.

"I'm not kidding," God said, not sounding very amused.

Joan closed her Bibles (five versions, not counting the paraphrase) and frowned at the ceiling. "Lord," she said, "that's simply out of the question. Min Niniver's the girl they call 'the Whale.' She must weigh three hundred pounds. If I were seen with her, I'd be a social outcast." She tossed her candy wrapper in the garbage. "And that would just *ruin* my witness!"

There was silence. Joan looked up at the ceiling again, but only saw the light fixture. To her surprise, God did not speak again.

In fact, she didn't hear a word from him—not even a postcard—for the next six months. Not that she worried about it too much. She was busy these days, and before she knew it she was ready to fly away to Upper Tarshishstan.

So she packed her suitcase full of missionary stuff and boarded a plane to the faraway land. But the Lord sent three skyjackers onto her flight, and halfway across the Atlantic Ocean they pulled out their guns and hand grenades. And everyone was sore afraid.

Everyone, that is, except Joan. She was sound asleep in her seat, next to a nervous hardware salesman from Trenton, New Jersey.

"Wake up!" cried the salesman, shaking Joan. "How can you sleep through this? We're being skyjacked!"

Joan opened her eyes. "What?" she mumbled.

"I notice you wear a cross," the salesman said frantically. "Maybe if you pray, we'll get out of this mess."

Joan brightened. "I'm glad you suggested that," she said,

Joan 'n' the Whale

whipping out her New Testament. "Let me witness to you." She proceeded to read thirty-four verses to the hardware salesman, as well as to a lady senator, two army generals, a baseball player, and several ministers. Before long, she had read her verses to nearly everyone on the plane.

Suddenly one of the skyjackers burst into the cabin. "Awright!" he yelled. "I want one hostage to keep with us. We're going to let the rest of you go."

The passengers cheered and pointed at Joan. "Take *her!*" they shouted in unison. A sigh of relief echoed up and down the aisles as she was led away.

Soon the plane landed, and the passengers were set free. But Joan was tied up in the cargo hold, and Joan was in the belly of the plane for three days and three nights.

Then Joan prayed to the Lord from the belly of the plane, saying, "Okay, God, I get the picture. If you get me out of here, I'll go back and witness to the Whale . . . I mean, to Min."

"Hold it," God said. "Who said anything about *witnessing?* I just said *friend.*"

"Gotcha."

The Lord spoke to the skyjackers, and they kicked Joan out upon the landing strip.

So Joan returned to her dorm room, and in a few months she was Min Niniver's friend. It took a lot of work, but lo and behold, after almost a year, Joan introduced Min to her friend God. The three of them became better friends than ever.

One day the word of the Lord came to Joan a second time, saying, "Joan, arise—"

"Oh, no," said Joan. "Where to this time?"

"Why, to Upper Tarshishstan, of course," said God.

"Ahhh," said Joan.

This time she took a boat.

5

The Final Frontier
of Alfred Centauri

*B*_{zzz.}

Blip.

Is this thing on? Okay.

Captain's log, Stardate 2217.6. Alfred Centauri recording.

Oh, forget it. I'm not the captain of the stupid starship. I'm just a crewman third class, and this is just my personal electronic diary. But Star Fleet *ought* to make me captain; the one they've got now is a real servo-droid. So is everybody else on this ship.

Except me, naturally.

Everything is wrong with this place. Take the programs, for instance—the computer programs. They're all so *boring*. They don't have any of my favorite cybernetic games, like Meteor Eater and Cosmic Catastrophe VII. All they've got is a bunch of stupid *space* stuff. Can you believe it? Who cares about *space*?

Yeah, yeah, we're orbiting Draconis IV, and there's exploring to be done. That's all they ever talk about—exploring strange new worlds, blah, blah, blah. I'm not into that stuff. But do they care? Ha! These guys don't seem to realize how lucky they are to have me on this trip at all. There are plenty of *other* starships in this galaxy, you know.

Then there are the other crew members. What a bunch of losers! They're all too short, tall, fat, skinny, loud, quiet. . . .

Joan 'n' the Whale

Why can't they be like me? If I'd known when I signed up for this voyage what a collection of space wimps would be aboard, I would've stayed home. At least there I didn't have to go to crew meeting all the time.

Crew meeting. What a joke. Who wants to go to the observation deck once a week to listen to Captain What's-his-name go on and on about how "great" it is to explore space? Who wants to sing those slow, boring songs about the Federation and read scraps of those moldy old Apollo flight logs?

Those meetings are duller than my nephew's black-hole collection. I just sit there and look at the ceiling or doodle pictures of antique jet cars in the margin of the songbook. Who cares about those old astronauts? I'd rather talk about important, interesting stuff—like that new 4-D Star Cannibals computer game or which team might win the next Intergalactic Time Travel Tournament. I didn't sign up for this trip to *learn* anything, after all.

Naturally, when I told one of the other crewmen what a disaster this voyage is, he was too dumb to catch on.

"What do you mean?" he asked. "Space exploration is fantastic! It's the best thing that ever happened to me. I didn't have any meaning in my life until I signed up with Star Fleet. Now I—"

"Yeah, yeah," I said, rolling my eyes. "I know. Now you're 'boldly going where no man has gone before.' "

"Right," he told me. "It's great to be a member of a crew, working together, exploring together. The crew needs us—and we need the crew. It's like one big life-support system!"

I groaned. What an asteroid brain! He'd swallowed that space garbage from the captain about how we have to stick together, help each other, work with the same "mission" in mind—sort of like "the parts of a well-oiled, ion-drive engine." Brother! How hokey can you get?

Well, I guess that's enough of this diary for tonight. I told that crewman what a Neptunian Slime Worm he was for going along with that "mission" stuff. Then I went to the game deck and found the only programs they have are dumb ones like Holographic Chess and Anti-Grav Bowling. *Everybody* has those. So I came back here to my cabin. At least here I don't have to listen to them sing "Upward Star Fleet Soldiers."

Guess I'll go to sleep now—if that stupid comet outside the window doesn't keep me awake. What a dump. Everywhere you look, space, space, and more space.

Centauri over and out for now.

Bzzz.
Blip.
Personal log, Stardate 2217.7. Alfred Centauri here. Okay, I've had it! I decided today that if nobody around here is going to pay attention to me and what *I* want, I'm just going to ignore *them*. *All* of them. Who needs 'em? Who needs their crew meetings and boring programs and Star Fleet classes? From now on I'm going to skip all that junk and do what *I* want to do. I'll show those nosecone heads what I think of their stupid "mission."

Well, time for bed. Nothing on the dining deck but sirloin steaks, baked potatoes, twelve kinds of salads, and banana splits—so I skipped dinner. Can't they get any *decent* food up here, like Tang? I'm thinking of giving up their lousy meals and just eating vitamins. That'll show 'em who's the *real* space cadet around here.

Over and out.

Bzzz.
Blip.
Personal log, Stardate 2217.9. Alfred Centauri reporting. Today I had to go down to the yucky planet's surface. What a waste of time! The dumb captain made his first mistake when he picked me for the landing party. Naturally he picked me last—the creep. He even got my name wrong— called me *Albert!* Can you believe it? Only four hundred

Joan 'n' the Whale

people on this ship, and he can't even remember my name!

So we had to go to the transporter room. Naturally there was room for everybody except me, so I had to beam down separately. I told the meteorhead at the transporter controls that he might as well beam me down about a hundred yards from the others, so I wouldn't have to listen to them go on and on about all that space junk. So what did he do? He beamed me into a stupid polymolecular *mudhole!*

Well, that was it. I whipped out my communicator and told that Plutonian Space Slug to beam me back up *now.* It took me a whole hour in the sonic shower to clean up—not that anybody *cared.*

The Final Frontier of Alfred Centauri

The rest of the landing party came back later and told everybody what great "adventures" they'd had, discovering ugly, smelly plants and picking up a load of dumb rocks. What a bunch of show-offs. They think they're so great, huh? Well, I've figured out a way to *really* show them, and tonight I'm going to do it.

Bzzz.

Blip.

Personal log, Stardate 2218.1. Centauri again. Boy, they're really going to learn their lesson this time. They think I'm going to hang around here forever just because of some dumb "mission," eh? Well, I'm going to show 'em I can do just fine on my own. Let *them* worry about putting up with each other, working on some common goal like a Saturnian ant colony. I've got a better way.

Let's see.... I'll just get my stuff together.... This tricorder and my vitamins and my *Twenty-First Century Trivia* book.... That's all I need.

I'll just walk out of my cabin ... down the corridor ... to air lock seven. I'll just press the button. That phony red light will go on, but that doesn't mean anything. Then I'll step into the air lock, and the door will shut all those airheads behind me at last.

I'll finally be free! No more boring meetings, no more dopey programs, no more having to tolerate a bunch of people I can't stand. Maybe I'll start my *own* crew out there. Yeah. You just wait—they'll be standing in line to join me!

Well, I'll continue this in the air lock. Stand by.

Bzzz.

Blip.

Personal log, Stardate 2218.2. Centauri speaking. Okay, I'm pushing the button. Now I'm—

Blip.

Bzzzzzzzzzzzzzzzzzzzzzzzzzzzzzzzzzzzzzzzzzzzzzzzzzzzzzzzzzzzzzzzzzzz.

6 Where Babies Come From ✍

Welcome, class, to biology 201. In the coming semester we'll be studying many things, but there's something I want to get out of the way right here and now. I'm talking about the question of where babies come from.

Now, hold on. I know this is a terribly controversial question and an emotional one. But this is a biology class, and we're going to deal with every subject in the clear, cold light of scientific fact. It's high time someone answered this question for you, once and for all!

Where do babies come from? It's an age-old problem that even the youngest people wonder about, and most adults are too untrained to answer scientifically. As a result, all kinds of old wives' tales have arisen on the subject. After all, when human beings are so ignorant of their very *beginnings*, they're bound to develop superstitions and legends to fill the gap.

But this is the era of frankness and honesty; let's not beat around the bush or feel embarrassed. Let us instead delve to the heart of this controversy.

Since the dawn of history, and no doubt before, man has tried to answer the question of where babies come from. Practically every culture on the globe has some "birth myth" in its earliest writings. The specifics of these myths vary, but for some reason a common thread runs through nearly all of them. And that thread has come to be known as *Childrenism*.

That's right—*children*. According to this primitive notion, babies come from "parents." In other words, babies are the "children" or "offspring" of adults. Yes, this theory sounds silly to us today. But we must remember that this explanation was concocted by people who had never heard of science or medicine or even aerosol cans. They worked with what they had, which was precious little indeed.

What? You want the details of Childrenism? Well, the specifics are hardly worth going into, except to say that it relied heavily on the idea of preexistent parents—that's right, adults who actually produced the baby! That in itself is enough to discredit the theory; after all, who were these parent beings, and how did *they* come to be? How could they have fabricated a baby? The whole idea sounds ridiculous and rightly so.

Now, class, settle down. To understand why the primitives believed in parents, we must realize that they desperately *wanted* to believe. According to Childrenism, parents were wonderful beings who produced babies as expressions of love, then lovingly cared for and protected the babies. Moreover, these parent beings were superior to babies in every way—stronger, taller, wiser, more self-sufficient. No wonder early man wanted to believe in parents; by doing so, he made the world seem like a more loving, safer place.

That's not all. Childrenism held that babies were brought forth in their parents' image. Thus early man could feel important and accepted, believing he was much like his preexistent, powerful "father" or "mother." Yes, it *is* pretty funny, isn't it?

Very well. We can see that while primitive man thought parents made babies, the exact opposite was true. Babies concocted the idea of parents. Unable to explain in scientific terms the strange, new world in which they found themselves, babies came up with the concept of Childrenism.

We might think that such an obviously wrong-minded theory would be quickly discarded, but that was hardly the case. For thousands of years Childrenism in its various forms prevailed, and countless other superstitions were based upon it.

But then came the Age of Enlightenment. Several courageous scientists broke with tradition and gave themselves to careful study of the question. They were jeered by the primitives, but labored on. Finally, after years of work, they answered the question that had intrigued humanity for eons.

Their answer came to be known as the Theory of Chance. Even today it is called a theory, though every respected scientist on the globe properly accepts it as absolute fact. A handful of primitives who still cling to Childrenism rail at the enlightened scientific community, but the civilized world has largely come around to the truth. That's why we're here today—to discover the truth.

So you ask, where *do* babies come from? Well, the Theory of Chance is rather complex, difficult for the untrained to fully grasp, but I can summarize it. Basically the theory explains that babies come to be through a variety of random means. There is no intelligent, powerful preexistent being who *produces* them; they just *happen.* For some, babies are brought by a large, long-legged bird called a *stork.* That's S-T-O-R-K. Here, I'll write it on the board. It is not clear where the stork comes from, though scientists are working on that; suffice it to say that the bird wraps the infant in a sling made of cloth, takes the ends of the cloth in its long beak, and flies with its burden to a populated area. There the bird chooses a house completely at random and drops the cloth-wrapped baby down the home's chimney, into the occupant's waiting arms.

For others the baby comes from a different source. Those who want to "have a baby" travel to an agricultural area and locate a cabbage patch. After obtaining the farmer's permission, the would-be baby possessors enter the cabbage patch and walk up and down the rows, looking under cabbage leaves. When an infant is found under one of the leaves, the adults pick it up and take it home with them.

Still others find a baby at the hospital. Arriving during visiting hours, the adults go to a place called the maternity ward, where a selection of infants is kept behind a large glass window. The adults line up in front of the window and choose a baby to take home with them, often picking one that they think resembles them. This is definitely the most expensive method, with the adults sometimes paying the hospital thousands of dollars for the infant of their choice.

Oh, there are other ways, all covered by the Theory of Chance. They include babies left in cradles by elves and fairies, babies deposited on doorsteps, and babies who grow on trees. The important thing to remember is that regardless of the means of arrival, babies just *happen*. Write that down. There is no rhyme or reason to the process and certainly no parent being who "creates" the "offspring." Such superstitions as Childrenism are best left where they belong—in the Dark Ages.

Well, that about wraps it up for today. What's that? No, my wife and I don't have any babies. No, I don't know why.

Any other questions? No? Class dismissed.

7

The Call 🌿

There was a Sitter, and there was a Stander.

The Sitter was smiling contentedly, reading a book as he sat at a sidewalk cafe. His sunglasses, Panama hat, tropical-print shirt, Bermuda shorts, and spotless white running shoes matched his mood of permanent leisure. An umbrella kept him in the shade; on the table at his elbow sat a tall glass of iced tea—and a shining white telephone.

Yawning, he slowly turned a page in his well-worn book. He was about to take a sip of the iced tea when he heard a voice.

"Hey!" cried the voice. He looked up. It was the Stander, and she was approaching his table. He frowned, but only for a moment, and went back to his reading.

"What do you know?" the girl greeted him, putting her hands on her hips. "Is that really you? Long time no see!"

"Hmmm," went the Sitter, not looking up.

"So what have you been doing all this time?" the girl asked.

The Sitter nodded toward his book, which he continued to read. "Studying, of course," he said proudly.

The girl scratched her head. "Studying? Well, I guess that's—" Glancing across the street, she gasped. "Hey!" she said. "What's going on over there?"

"Hmmm?" the Sitter murmured.

"An old man just fell down in the crosswalk," she said urgently. "Come on, we'd better go help him!" She ran off, leaving the Sitter reading in the shade. Slowly he turned another page; it was his only movement.

A minute later the Stander returned, panting from her dash. "Well," she said between breaths, "he's okay." She frowned. "Hey, how come you didn't give me a hand?"

Irritated, he looked up from his book. "Because I'm waiting, of course," he said.

"Waiting for *what?*" she asked.

"For the Call," he replied, nodding at the phone on the table.

The Stander shook her head. "What's the—" Just then she happened to look down a nearby alley. "Look!" she cried. "That kid just snatched a lady's purse. Come on—we can probably catch him!" Off she ran again, and the Sitter just sat.

Two minutes later she was back, huffing and puffing. "Hey," she said. "What kind of neighborhood *is* this? People falling in the streets, kids snatching purses. . . . What's the matter with you? Why didn't you come with me?"

The Sitter lifted his head and glared. "Because I didn't get the Call!"

"What call?" the girl asked, exasperated.

"The Call," he answered, looking skyward.

The girl threw up her hands. "I don't—" All at once she noticed something else down the street. "Oh, did you see that?" she asked, putting her hand to her mouth. "That car just took a left and plowed right into the motorcycle. Now, come on! Don't just sit there; we've got to help!"

The Sitter sipped his iced tea. "I'm sorry," he said, unconcerned. "But I'm just not called."

The girl started to run in the direction of the accident. "What are you studying, anyway?" she shouted at him over her shoulder.

"First aid," he said placidly and returned to his reading.

Three minutes later the girl was back, so exhausted she could barely stand. "I've got to use your phone," she said, gasping for breath.

"What?" the Sitter cried, suddenly alert.

"I've got to call an ambulance for that guy," she panted and reached for the shining white telephone.

The Sitter leaped from his chair, wrestling the phone away. "You can't do that!" he said, his eyes panicky. "Why, the Call could come at any time! I might get the Call any *minute* now!"

All at once it happened. *Rrrinnngggg,* went the telephone.

The sound froze the Sitter and the Stander in their tracks. Time itself seemed to pause as the Sitter looked down at the phone in his arms.

He swallowed. "I—oh, my," he said, trembling. "It's—it's finally happened. . . . Oh, what an honor! I've finally received . . . the *Call!*"

Carefully, gingerly, he picked up the receiver. "Yes?" he breathed into the mouthpiece.

For a moment he listened. Then he took the receiver from his ear and stared at it, anger gathering on his face.

"I don't believe it!" he cried, thrusting the receiver at the girl. "It's—it's for *you!*"

Grabbing his iced tea and his first-aid manual, the Sitter stalked off. The Stander chatted cheerily with the voice on the wire, as if she had been listening to it all her life.

8 Account Your Blessings🌿

*W*_{here is that guy?} wondered Christopher Carper nervously, pacing back and forth in his living room. He paused long enough to part the front window curtains and check the driveway. No one was there, so he started pacing again.

They're gonna nail me this time for sure, he thought. *I just know it.* Perspiration popped out on his forehead as visions of policemen, handcuffs, and prison bars spun through his brain.

"What am I thinking?" he whispered and stopped. "I haven't done anything wrong. Have I?" Once more he looked out the window. Nothing.

It's just that I've never been . . . audited . . . before. He walked to the dinette table and readjusted the pile of papers there for the seventh or eighth time. *I hope he's impressed with these records. Took me two days to get together—*

Just then the doorbell rang. "Aaugh!" Christopher Carper yelled, and the papers in his hands went flying in ten different directions. In vain he tried to restraighten them, then gave up. Reluctantly he walked to the door, hoping the November cold had somehow permanently frozen the lock.

But it was not to be. The door opened, revealing an official-looking—but attractive—young woman. She carried an official-looking but attractive briefcase.

"Mr. Christopher Carper?" she asked briskly.

Christopher Carper stared. "No . . . uh, yes!" he stammered. "I mean, I just didn't expect. . . . Are you—?"

"I'm Miss Wickersham from the Eternal Revenue Service," she announced. "The ERS would like me to conduct a routine audit of your records."

He tried to remember what to say, but nothing came to mind. "Er . . . yes, of course," he finally managed. "I mean, come right in!"

She did so and followed him to the table. "I—I've never been audited by the Eternal Revenue Service before," he said, attempting a chuckle that came out rather weakly. "I'm . . . well, I'm a good guy. . . . I think—"

"There's no need to be nervous, Mr. Carper," she said, opening her briefcase on the paper-strewn table. "The ERS has chosen your name at random. After examining your thanks return, we'd like to know why you gave so little thanks last year."

He swallowed, watching her take a large printing calculator from the briefcase. "I . . . uh . . . I'm as thankful as the next guy," he offered. "It's just that—well, it was a *terrible* year."

"That's what we're here to determine, Mr. Carper," said Miss Wickersham. She switched the calculator on, and it went *beeep*. "We have records, too, you know," she added.

He sat down across from her. "I see," he said. "You want to . . . count my blessings, so to speak." He forced a laugh. "Get it? 'Count your blessings'?"

"You might put it that way, Mr. Carper," she said politely but firmly. "*Account* might be more accurate. Let's begin, shall we?"

"Yes, let's," he said, feeling numb.

"Now, then. I see from our records that on January 24 of last year you received a substantial raise in salary." *Beep* went the calculator as she pressed a button.

Account Your Blessings   45

"Oh, yeah," he said, remembering. "I was very thankful about that. I looked up," he added, looking up, "and said, 'Thanks.' "

Miss Wickersham frowned slightly. "I see," she said and pushed another button. *Beep.*

She looked at her list again. "And on March 3 you recovered from a serious illness. . . ."

Carper squinted, thinking. "I must have been thankful. Why, sure! It was a miracle of medical science!"

Beep went the calculator. He gulped.

"Between June 19 and July 1, you camped out in Montana. Our records show it didn't rain once."

"Uh, right," he said. "Some good luck, huh?"

Beep.

"Oh," he muttered.

"On September 7, you sold a house for $5,000 more than you expected to get. To what did you attribute that turn of events?"

He shrugged. "Good business sense?" he ventured.

"Mr. Carper," said Miss Wickersham, looking over the top of her glasses, "I'm afraid you failed to declare a significant number of blessings last year."

He shook his head vigorously. "That can't be," he protested. "I've got *excellent* records!" He gathered up the sheaf of papers, trying to put them in some kind of order.

"For the month of January alone, here are blessings you are listed in our records as receiving," she said, consulting her notebook. The calculator's *beep* punctuated her reading of each entry as Carper frantically searched his papers. "New shoes, enjoyed watching a sunset, didn't slip on the ice walking home from church, medium-rare steak turned out as ordered, lettuce went on sale, phone call from an old friend, got in a car accident—"

He sat up straight. "Hey, wait a minute. 'Got in a car accident'? I'm supposed to be thankful for *that?*"

"Mr. Carper," Miss Wickersham said sincerely, "we

have a motto at the Eternal Revenue Service: 'In all things give thanks.'"

He groaned.

"No serious injury in car accident," she continued. "Found house keys you had lost—"

"Wait," he cried, holding up his hand. "You've got a list longer than my arm, and we're still on January! Can't you just tell me what the—uh—bottom line of all this is?"

Miss Wickersham ripped the paper tape from the calculator and looked it over. "Well, Mr. Carper," she said at length, "it seems you owe a great deal of thanks."

Christopher Carper lowered his head. Images of judges and jails marched through his mind. "Oh," he moaned. "I knew this would happen. What will you do now? Throw me in prison? Make me pay for the rest of my life?"

Miss Wickersham was silent as she switched off her calculator and returned it to her briefcase. Then she put her notebook in the case and snapped it shut.

"No, Mr. Carper," she said finally. "My work here is finished."

"You mean somebody *else* is coming to take me away?" he mourned, covering his eyes with his hands.

"No, no. You're free to go, to stay—to do as you please."

He sat up. *"Free?"* he said. "How? I thought I flunked the audit." He stared at her as she walked toward the door.

She turned to face him. "Giving thanks is voluntary, Mr. Carper," she said gently. "It has to come from the heart."

He pinched himself to make sure he wasn't dreaming. Then he started to laugh, relieved. "Well, of course!" he said, leaping to his feet and following her to the door. "Why, I couldn't agree more!" He waved his arm magnanimously. "I tell you what I'll do. I'll make it all up to you. To show how thankful I am, I'll ... uh ... I'll eat a great big dinner! Yeah! A huge turkey dinner with dressing and cranberries and sweet potatoes. . . ."

An almost imperceptible sigh escaped Miss Wickersham's lips. "Thank you for your time, Mr. Carper," she said as she left, sounding a little tired.

"No, thank *you*," said Christopher Carper, closing the door behind her. He could almost taste that pumpkin pie already.

9

The New Ump

The crowd was going crazy. The score stood at eight to seven by the start of the ninth inning, and even the hot dog vendors were starting to turn from their hawking to watch the championship battle on the diamond. Hats, paper cups, and souvenir programs bobbed in the air as the evenly divided spectators cheered their teams toward victory.

The umpire, a white-haired veteran whose eyes twinkled behind his face mask, whisked dust from home plate as the visiting team took the field. He was about to yell, "Play ball!" when something happened.

"Attention," said an official-sounding voice over the public-address system. "Umpire substitution."

"What?" asked several people in the stands. "What did he say?"

"Umpire substitution," repeated the voice. "The old umpire will be replaced for the remainder of the game."

"*Replace* him?" a fan cried. "Why? He's done a great job all these years. He's called 'em fairly today, too."

But all the voice would say was, "New ump, please take your position."

With that a new umpire took his place behind home plate. He looked like the old umpire—same dark blue chest pad, same black pants, same white hair. But he was different somehow.

"You're *out*," the new ump told his predecessor, jerking a thumb toward the showers. The old umpire shook his head sadly at the crowd, then walked slowly toward the stadium exit.

"Play ball!" the new ump shouted, and players took their positions. The crowd, forgetting its momentary puzzlement, resumed yelling and throwing things.

The pitcher wound up, then let a curve ball fly over the plate. The batter didn't move. Everyone waited for the new ump to yell, "Strike!" but he said nothing.

"Well?" the batter asked impatiently. "Was it a strike or a ball?" Players and spectators watched curiously as the new ump scratched his chin.

"Well, that all *depends*," the umpire said. "I'd hate to set myself up as a judge, after all." Everyone stared as he meticulously swept off the plate again.

"*Wait* a minute," cried the coach of the home team, leaping from his bench. "Are you trying to tell me you can't decide whether that was a ball or a strike? The *old* ump could have decided!"

The new ump frowned. "That's precisely why we had to get rid of him," he said. "The old ump was hopelessly out of date, always imposing his beliefs on others. He acted as though everything were black and white—a strike or a ball, a safe or an out. Times have changed; we modern people know better."

"We *do*?" the other coach asked.

"Of course," the new ump said. "These are gray areas. One man's safe is another man's out. Now, play ball— please."

Confused, the players and coaches took their places again. Once more the pitcher wound up and threw—this time a fast ball. The batter swung and connected with a loud *crack*.

"A base hit!" cried the home coach as his half of the crowd cheered.

"No way!" the other coach declared as the ball hit the ground. "It's a foul!"

The coaches approached each other, fists clenched, and for ten minutes bellowed their debate. Finally one of them said hoarsely, "Let's ask the umpire."

"Oh, my," the ump said, pressing his fingertips together thoughtfully. "Who's to say what's foul and what isn't? I certainly can't. The courts can't come up with a definition. In some countries, what's foul is fair, and what's fair is—"

"*I* know a foul when I see it!" one of the coaches shouted.

"So do I!" yelled the other.

"Gentlemen, *gentlemen*," the umpire said. "You're being *subjective*. One person's word is as good as another's." He smiled soothingly.

"Hold it," the home coach protested, pulling a rolled-up pamphlet from his back pocket. "Here's the rulebook. We've always gone by the rulebook."

The umpire stifled a snicker. "Oh, *that* old thing," he said.

"Nobody believes in it anymore. It's a collection of misinformation."

"It *is?*" the coaches asked, surprised.

"Why, that book is chock-full of mistakes," the ump replied. "For one thing, it doesn't tell how baseballs are manufactured, which proves it's unscientific. It's been around since Abner Doubleday. Who knows how many errors have been added as it's been handed down?"

"Wow, I never thought of it that way before," the visiting coach said.

The home coach frowned. "But if the rulebook is no good, how can we come up with a way to play the game?"

The umpire smiled. "Why, democratically, of course. We'll just have the fans *vote* every time we need a rule. Go along with the crowd, so to speak."

Shrugging, the coaches returned to their dugouts. "Play ball!" the new ump cried again.

The pitcher let fly another fast ball, high and inside. When the batter failed to swing, the ump turned to the crowd. "Let's vote," he yelled. "How many think that was a strike?"

An affirmative roar went up from half the fans. The other half booed.

"And how many thought that was a ball?" the ump asked.

The second half screamed approval, while the first half growled.

"It was a strike, idiot!" a fan yelled.

"Any fool could see it was a ball!" shouted another.

Suddenly someone threw a popcorn box, and a fistfight broke out. Within seconds the stands were a surging mass of punching and kicking.

"I quit!" announced the pitcher, hurling his glove to the ground. "What's the use of pitching, if nobody will call the strikes?"

"I quit, too," said the batter. "No point in hitting if foul and fair are the same thing." He flung his bat away in disgust, hitting the other team's pitcher.

"Ow!" the pitcher cried, and before long the dugouts were packed with players trying to strangle each other.

"Stop!" shouted the home coach over the din. "There's only one way to resolve this. We've got to get the old umpire back!"

There was a pause in the commotion as fans and players turned their ears to the coach. But then the coach frowned.

"On second thought," he worried, "the old ump would probably throw us *all* out of the stadium now, the way we're acting. So let's not."

"Yeah!" screamed the crowd and players, resuming their battle.

The new umpire finished his plate dusting and looked up at the chaos raging around him. "Uh—play ball?" he said uncertainly.

Nobody was listening.

10 The Macedonian Call

*R*rringgg. *Rrringgg. Click.*

"Good afternoon—Apostolic Talent Associates, home of the really big names in early Christendom. Sam Sapphira speaking. How may I minister unto you?"

"Uh . . . I'm calling from Macedonia. We need somebody to come over here and help us."

"Help in Macedonia, eh? Hmmm. . . . I think I've got just the thing for you, Mr . . . Mr—"

"Flavius. What we need, Mr. Sapphira, is someone to come over and—"

"Listen, Flavius, I know just what you need. Oh, and call me Sam, okay?"

"Okay."

"Now, Flavius, let me guess your situation. You've got a fairly new church, and you're not packing 'em in like the one in Jerusalem. You need to spice up your program, maybe bring in a week of special speakers or a Christian theatrical troupe or something. I've got a comic who does stand-up routines about the bunch who won't eat meat offered to idols—"

"Uh, no, Mr . . . Sam. We're not a new church."

"I see. Well, then, you must be an old church. You're looking for a revival, right? You need some former heathens who went through spectacular conversions. I've got a former Roman centurion who gave it all up to become a follower, and a woman who was into soothsaying. How does that sound?"

"Well, actually, we're looking for something else."

"I don't get it, Flavius. Is it the summer slump? You need a musical group to bring 'em in on a Saturday night? If you want the youth crowd, we can book Children of the Catacombs—they've got an album coming out any day now."

"To tell you the truth, Sam, we're not a church at all. The Gospel hasn't reached Macedonia yet—so there aren't any churches here."

"No churches? Well, what can I do about that? That means you haven't got a decent sound system or *anything.*"

"Well, we were hoping you could send someone to preach the Gospel here."

"Oh, wow, Flavius, I don't know. I'm pretty low on evangelists right now. I do have Brother Benjy Braggadocios, but he prefers to evangelize people who are already saved. . . ."

"Well, we were hoping the Apostle Paul could come and help us."

"Paul? Oh, man, do you realize what you're asking? Paul is simply *the* evangelist of our day! I couldn't ask him to travel to some backwater district where there aren't even any churches."

"But I thought he did that sort of thing all the time."

"Well, frankly, I'm not up on everything the guy does. To be perfectly honest with you, Apostolic Talent Associates doesn't officially have Paul under contract. I did meet him in Jerusalem once, but let me tell you, I don't know why he's so popular. He's got about as much charisma as a piece of unleavened bread."

"But, Sam, we really would like to have Paul. We believe the Lord wants him to do a great work here."

"Right, right. You and every other guy in the known world. Paul's a busy man, Flavius. You can't expect him to drop his carefully planned missionary journeys and make a detour to Macedonia. Besides, he's probably too expensive for you. He's always hauling Silas and Luke and sometimes even Timothy around with him. Think of the upkeep, the expenses."

"Well . . . we don't have much money here. . . ."

"Exactly. You've got to be realistic in this business, Flavius, believe me. Now let's see what I can do for you. We've got a few people who are willing to work outdoors, and they won't break your budget. How about the Singing Cyrenes? They were a smash at Antioch. Or maybe a guy who does object lessons with spears? We've also got a team of distance runners who hand out tracts as they go through town. . . ."

"I—I don't think so, Sam. I guess the only person we really want is Paul. We feel strongly that God wants him to help us."

"Hmm. Boy, Flavius, you're a stubborn man. I tell you what I'll do. I hear Paul and his party are in Phrygia and Galatia at the moment. But when they get back, I'd be willing to try to contact him and see what I can do."

"Really? Oh, Sam, that would be wonderful."

"Of course, you realize that for someone of Paul's caliber we'd have to require a minimum guarantee from you."

"A what?"

"A guarantee. You know, the number of paid admissions you'd promise to provide. That way we're sure we won't lose money."

"Paid admissions? But we were planning to let everybody listen for free."

"*Free?* Oh, heh-heh. Now I know you're kidding me, Flavius."

"No, really. We couldn't charge people to hear the Gospel."

"Oh, man. I'm afraid you got a wrong number, Flavius. If you're going to have that attitude, we can't do business. This is the real world, pal, not fantasyland."

"I—I see. Well, I'm sorry I bothered you, Mr. Sapphira. Thank you for your time."

"Oh, come on, Flavius. I hate to see you go away empty-handed. For next to nothing I can get you a traveling multi-media show about the Day of Pentecost. How does that grab you?"

"No, I'm sorry."

"Okay, Flavius, have it your way. But I warn you, you'll never get the Apostle Paul to come to Macedonia."

"Perhaps we can reach him in some other way. The Lord will take care of it."

"Dream on, Flavius."

"Say, that's it! Thanks for the idea, Mr. Sapphira, and good-bye."

"Huh? What did I say?"

Click.

11 The Great Maxwell Machmaster

Yeah, that *other* guy used to be my best friend. You know—the one who sees everything you do and never wants to do anything fun. What a drag.

Anyway, I dumped him. It was the smartest thing I ever did, because that's when I found out what a *real* friend is.

That's when I met ... the Great Maxwell Machmaster!

What? You say you don't *know* Max? Well, he's just the neatest guy who ever lived, that's all! My *old* friend probably wouldn't approve of him, but then that guy didn't approve of *anything*. Max is—well, let me tell you what a great friend he's been to me. Then I *know* you'll understand. . . .

I first met Max back in high school. When I came into class one day at the start of the year, all the kids were sticking their heads out the window, yelling.

"Go, Max!" one shouted. "Way to be, buddy!" another yelled. I looked out the window, and there was this tall, skinny guy on the ledge. The ledge wasn't even a foot wide, but this guy was balancing there, four stories off the ground, on tiptoe—on a roller skate. As if that weren't enough, he was blindfolded and juggled a handful of double-edged razor blades!

Wow! I thought. *What a guy!* Since I was in the market for a new best friend, I was keeping an eye out for likely candi-

The Great Maxwell Machmaster

dates. The guy on the ledge obviously belonged at the top of my list; he was intelligent, popular, and knew how to have a good time. Not like my *former* friend, who never would have had the brains to juggle razor blades on a fourth-floor ledge.

I watched as the guy they called Max climbed back into the room amid the class's applause. Not only was this Max smart, he was a snappy dresser. He looked a lot like Indiana Jones in *Raiders of the Lost Ark*, except that his old leather flight jacket was scorched in spots and full of holes, and his hat looked as if it had been chewed by wild dogs. He even had a few whiskers on his chin.

Talk about mature! I thought. *Think how much he could teach me about clothes, grooming, and personal hygiene!*

Right then I decided: This was the guy. The question was: Would *he* want to be *my* best friend?

At lunchtime I headed for the cafeteria to look for him. By now I'd found out that his name was Maxwell J. Machmaster, and that his really good friends got to call him Max. *Man, I'd give anything to be able to call him that*, I thought wistfully.

A small crowd was gathering in the cafeteria when I got there. "What's going on?" I asked a guy on the edge of the group.

"It's Max," he said excitedly. "He's about to break another world record—eating brown paper lunch sacks!" Sure enough, Max was tearing lunch bags into little pieces, then swallowing them.

What a great guy! I thought. Not only was he a genius, an athlete, and a fashion expert—he was a gourmet, too! Not like my *old* friend, who never wanted me to eat anything but *food*.

"That's fifteen!" a girl squealed as Max polished off the last sack. He burped as the bell rang, and the crowd cheered.

Slowly they drifted away, leaving the great man to dig

shreds of paper from his teeth, with a toothpick. Trembling, I finally worked up the nerve to approach him.

"Uh—hi," I managed.

He belched.

"Uh—I'm kind of new around here," I began, "and I was sort of wondering if . . . uh. . . ."

"Yeah, yeah, I know," he said, sounding disgusted. "You want to be my best friend. Everybody does." He pulled a little black appointment book from his pocket and glanced at it.

"I think I can fit you in on Thursday night at 10:45," he muttered.

I gulped. "That's kind of late, isn't it?" I asked. "I'm not sure—"

"Take it or leave it," he said, snapping his little book shut. "Do you want to be my best friend or not?"

"Of *course* I do," I blurted. "Who wouldn't? I mean, you must be the neatest guy who ever lived. Not like my old—"

"I don't want to hear about your old friend," Max said abruptly. "Meet me on the football field Thursday night. Now, get lost!"

Man, I thought, walking dazedly away. *What a guy!* I could hardly believe it. *I* was going to be a friend of *the* Maxwell Machmaster! What would my old friend think of that? He probably couldn't even *imagine* anybody as great as the Great Maxwell Machmaster.

It seemed to take forever for Thursday night to come, but it finally did. I walked to the football field, and sure enough, there was Max, sitting in the bleachers. He was still wearing his Indiana Jones outfit, and in his hand was a paper bag. For a second I thought he was going to break his sack-eating record again, but then I saw the outline of a bottle in the bag.

"Okay, whoever you are," he said as I approached. "You want to be my best friend? Then take a drink." He pulled a plastic bottle with a nozzle cap out of the bag.

I gasped. "But that's *detergent!*" I said. "You can't drink that stuff. It's not good for you."

He sneered. "*Good* for you? Did your *old* friend tell you that?"

"Uh, no," I lied. "I just thought—"

"*All* my friends like to drink," he hissed and put the bottle to his lips. After a long swallow he burped again, and soap bubbles floated from his mouth.

"Here, idiot," he said, handing the bottle to me. "Now *you* drink—if you *really* want to be my best friend, that is."

For a second I actually almost forgot what a great guy Max was. Isn't that crazy? But then I came to my senses and knew what I had to do. I grabbed the bottle and took a drink.

For some reason I felt as if I was turning green. "G-g-great stuff," I said, when I could finally speak. "Y-you sure know how to have fun, Max."

"That's *Mr.* Machmaster to you, jerk," he said. "Now, let's have some smoke. You *are* into smoke, aren't you? *All* my best friends are."

I swallowed. My *old* friend had warned me about smoke, too. But he was just old-fashioned. He'd never had a great friend like Maxwell J. Machmaster!

"Sure, I'm into smoke," I said, following Max behind the bleachers to where he had parked his dented red sportscar with the flame decals. He fastened a rubber hose to the car's tail pipe, then turned on the engine.

"Take a whiff of this," he commanded, sticking the hose in my face. A hot, thick cloud of exhaust hit my nostrils, gagging me.

"Hmmm," Max said as I went into a coughing fit. "Are you *sure* you've got what it takes to be my best friend?"

"Uh, yeah—yes!" I croaked, still choking.

Just then Max looked at his watch. "Your time's up, moron," he said.

"Am—am I your friend yet?" I asked, coughing.

"You've got a long way to go," he said. "Next week we'll go over more of the basics—like sleeping in the middle of the freeway, swimming in the sewer, setting your hair on fire. Stuff like that."

"Wow," I said. "You—you're really some kind of guy."

"You ain't seen nothin' yet," he told me. "Later you'll get into the *really* great stuff, like driving your car over a cliff and injecting yourself with a fatal disease." He checked his watch impatiently.

"What a guy," I murmured. "What a guy!"

"Now, take a hike," he said, chugging down the last of the detergent. "My *friends* don't bore me."

"Y-yes, sir," I said. "Right away, sir!" I turned and ran down the street, ecstatic. What a night! With hard work and plenty of time, maybe I *could* be a best friend of the Great Maxwell Machmaster. I could hardly wait for next Thursday night!

Now, years later, Max lets me call him by his first name. Boy, was I excited when he said I could do that! He even gives me an extra fifteen minutes once a month so we can do neater stuff than ever.

My *old* friend was such a zero. He could probably never see how fantastic it is that, since I met the Great Maxwell Machmaster, I've broken both arms three times, singed all my hair off, lost one leg and four fingers, and even caught malaria twice. What are friends for, right?

But I know *you* understand, now that I've told you about the Great Maxwell Machmaster.

Don't you?

12

The Parable
of the Talents ✑

It came to pass that a Master had 300 servants; and the Master, who was about to embark upon a long journey, called his servants together and entrusted talents to each of them. To some he gave one talent, to others two, to others three or more. But each servant—short or tall, clever or dull, trained or untrained—received at least one talent.

Some received the talent of singing, some dancing, some painting pictures of waterfalls in the moonlight. Others were talented in public speaking, baking cookies, pushing children up and down on the playground swings, or visiting the sick. Still others received talents enabling them to collect money, vacuum the floor, or teach.

"I am going on a long journey," the Master said when he had finished handing out talents. "As my servants, work wisely with the talents I have given you." With that, he left.

"Very well," said one of the servants, a fellow who had the talent of organization. "Let us band together in our Master's service, using these talents to do the work he has left us." He pointed at a servant who had the talent of speaking the Master's words. "You will remind us of what the Master has said. Those of you who have musical talents will sing to us of the Master and his work."

So it went, and before long each servant was given something to do according to his or her talent. Some cared for

Joan 'n' the Whale

servants who were old or ill, some brought water to those who toiled in the Master's orchards, some invited strangers into their homes and made them feel welcome, and some taught others about the Master and his goodness.

Soon a group of servants who could use hammers and saws built a meeting house for the benefit of all, and those who were talented in making furniture and sewing curtains furnished it. People came from miles around to the meeting house to hear of the Master and honor him.

For a while the Master's work flourished, but one day a change occurred. A servant who was talented in mending shoes decided his task wasn't important enough.

"I want to do something important," he complained, "like singing or speaking the Master's words in the meeting house. Mending shoes is for nobodies."

"But mending shoes *is* important," another servant said. "Wouldn't it be harder to do the Master's work in bare feet?"

"That's not *my* problem," the discontented worker replied. "I want a more important place. Those singers and speakers we've got now aren't so talented anyway."

The servant whose talent was mending shoes promptly stopped exercising his talent. Before long the other servants' shoes began to leak, and they became discontented, too.

"I'm tired of working with wet feet," said one. "Let's hire a shoemaker."

"I want a more important job, too," chimed in another. "Placing long-distance phone calls to the Master isn't very exciting."

"Yeah," agreed still another. "I'm tired of inviting strangers into my home. Let somebody else do it."

Soon the length and breadth of the Master's property was in an uproar. Some servants refused to exercise their talents, while others demanded a more exalted place. Some accused others of laziness or being puffed up or requiring too much work. Still others said that certain talents should not be exercised, that perhaps the Master had not meant to give them at all. When the Master's business had finally ground to a halt, the servant who had the talent of organization called an emergency gathering in the meeting house.

"All right!" he cried over the noise. "The Master's plan for us to carry out his work according to the talents he gave us is obviously not going to work. Therefore we will make the following changes:

"One: The speakers of the Master's words will also visit the sick, teach outsiders about the Master, sing, talk to strangers, and perform organizational duties. But their most important task will be to try to convince the rest of us to work, too.

"Two: Should a servant decide to work, his job will be determined by what he feels like doing and how convincing the speaker of the Master's words has been. Servants are welcome to keep their talents, but need not feel obligated to exercise them."

The servant whose talent was organization left the platform, surrounded by the cheers of the congregated servants. The few speakers of the Master's words reluctantly took on their new responsibilities, and the rest of the people went home.

The new plan was immensely popular, but before long the trees in the orchard stopped bearing quite so much fruit. Weeds grew around the meeting house, and attendance at the meetings dwindled. Fewer strangers heard about the Master and his goodness, and the servants began to get used to walking around in leaky shoes.

There were some servants who faithfully continued at their tasks, often having to pretend they possessed others' talents. Many, however, having time on their hands, put their talents to other uses.

Instead of welcoming strangers into their homes, they gave elaborate parties for friends. Instead of visiting the sick, they went on vacations to faraway places. Rather than singing about the Master, they collected recordings of others who did it for them.

The servant whose talent was organization kept right on exercising his talent, making lists of potential workers for the speakers of the Master's words to cajole. But the weeds grew longer, and the orchard's harvest grew smaller every year.

By the time the Master returned from his journey, only a few servants were still at their posts. The speakers of the Master's words were exhausted from overwork, and the harvest filled only half as many bushel baskets as before.

"What happened?" the Master cried to the assembled servants, a mixture of anger and sadness in his voice. "What happened to the talents I entrusted to you?"

"We—we buried them," came the reply.

You should have seen the Master's face.

13

F ood was a very serious matter to Arthur S. Nob. Sunday morning, Sunday evening, and midweek meals were especially important, but the choice of a restaurant was the most crucial element of all.

Other people seemed content simply to pick a restaurant, get their food, and start chomping away, but not Arthur. He was a gourmet, and proud of it. The restaurant *he* went to had to be *perfect*.

So it was that when he moved to Midleyville, disillusioned with the restaurants in the last town, he plunked down his suitcases and cardboard cartons in the middle of the living room and ran to look at the Yellow Pages.

Restaurants, he read, and ran his finger down the list. "Quite a choice," he muttered, "and probably not a decent one among them." Nevertheless, he had to try. Putting the phone book under his arm and checking his wallet for his Diner's Club card, he set out in his flawlessly polished Lincoln to find the perfect eating establishment.

The first place he came to was, appropriately enough, called the First Restaurant of Midleyville. From his car, with a jaundiced eye, Arthur beheld the large brick building. "Unimaginative architecture," he mumbled. "Lettering on the sign is outdated. And I just *loathe* those shrubs." He shook his head. "Obviously not the restaurant for me." With that he drove on.

The next establishment was called Josephson's. Arthur pulled into the parking lot and gave it the once-over. "Hmmm," he said. "Rustic decor. Not outstanding, but not *gauche* either." He got out of his car and sighed. "I probably won't like it, but I'll check it out."

Inside, a smiling hostess met him. "Party of one?" she asked.

Arthur's eyes narrowed. "I don't like the way you said that," he said suspiciously. "It's none of your business if I'm a party of one. Are you insinuating that I have no friends?"

"Why—why, of course not, sir," the hostess replied, flustered. "I merely wanted to know—"

"Humph," said Arthur. "If there's anything I can't stand, it's nosy restaurant people. Just for that, I won't be dining here after all." The hostess stared as Arthur turned on his heel and left.

"Party of one, indeed," Arthur murmured as he drove on. "A little too familiar, if you ask me. A restaurant should be friendly, but not *too* friendly." Frowning, he turned a corner and found a third place, the Family Diner.

This time there was no hostess to meet him. PLEASE SEAT YOURSELF, said a sign on the wall.

"Ridiculous," Arthur cried. "I demand service!"

"Can I help you, sir?" asked a waitress, coming over to him.

"I doubt it," Arthur said with a sniff. "This restaurant is obviously not interested in attracting newcomers. As a visitor, I expect to be greeted warmly—though not *too* warmly. Since you don't seem to want my business very badly, you shall not get it!" He walked out.

The next place was the Midleyville Community Steak House. Rating the decor as barely passing, Arthur was seated by a waiter and handed a menu. But before he could open it, he observed a young couple at a nearby table. They were both wearing brightly colored Hawaiian-print shirts.

Arthur's face reddened with anger. "Waiter!" he shouted, and the waiter hurried over. "Do you mean to tell me,"

Arthur hissed, "that you allow people wearing Hawaiian-print shirts to enter your restaurant?"

"Well, yes," the waiter replied nervously. "They need to eat, too, don't they?"

Arthur stood up. "I've never seen such an outrageous thing in my life," he growled. Tossing the menu on the table, he stalked out.

"Aren't there any decent restaurants in this town?" he cried, pulling onto the street. "Poor architecture, ugly decor, nosy hostesses, unfriendly atmosphere, low-class patrons—a man could *starve* in this place."

Down the street he spotted another restaurant, the Mustard Seed. *Ugh*, he thought, *one of those health-food places*. But then he took a closer look, and saw STEAKS, SEAFOOD, HOMEMADE PIES on the sign.

The architecture, decor, service, and patrons passed Arthur's muster. But he was scowling at the menu when the waitress came to take his order.

"This menu is a *disaster*," he said, wrinkling up his nose. "You offer no special programs for age groups, such as free balloons for children or discounts for senior citizens. You have no variety—only a choice of baked, boiled, french fried, or mashed potatoes with the steaks, no *au gratin*. There is little foreign emphasis—no kangaroo-tail soup or frog's legs. Even your live music is unacceptable."

"I'm sorry, sir," the waitress said. "But there's so much that *is* on the menu. Isn't there anything you'd like?"

Arthur snorted. "That's not the point," he answered icily. "Everything must be just so if I am to dine here. I am a *gourmet*. I demand that the menu be changed to fit my specifications, or I shall be forced to go elsewhere."

The waitress looked at him helplessly. "Very well," Arthur said. "I shall take my business somewhere else—where I will be appreciated."

By now his stomach was making horrendous grinding noises. "Quiet," he commanded. "I am a gourmet, not a starving derelict. I will not be pressured into accepting a restaurant that is less than *perfect*."

The sounds continued, but Arthur kept his nose in the air—passing such places as the King's Platter, the Last Supper, and the Bread and Vine. "They're not right, any of them," he said bitterly. "There's only one possibility left—a place called the Food Fellowship near the edge of town. If *that* doesn't work, I'll just have to go hungry."

He eased into a parking space and looked the place over. "So far, so good." He spoke cautiously. "Tastefully appointed." Inside the service was excellent.

Arthur opened the menu, then raised his eyebrows. *Impressive*, he thought. *But how does the food taste?*

When his dinner came, he was overcome by the rich fragrance of perfectly prepared cuisine. His tastebuds exulted as he partook of the Caesar salad, the veal *cordon bleu*, the delicately seasoned rice pilaf. For dessert he savored a delicious chocolate mousse, then relaxed with a cup of espresso.

"Waiter," he called happily when he had finished the sumptuous repast. "Seldom have even *I* enjoyed such a faultless banquet. I must personally give my compliments to the chef."

"Very well, sir," the waiter said, bowing graciously. "I shall bring him from the kitchen."

"Ah," Arthur exclaimed when the chef appeared in a few moments, his white hat bobbing as he bowed. "Chef, you have my compliments on a marvelous meal. I shall dine here every Sunday morning, Sunday evening, and Wednesday night, as well as on special occasions. I shall faithfully pay my bill and even leave a tip. In return I require only a few things of you."

"Oh?" the chef asked.

"As chef of this restaurant, you will serve only dishes that I enjoy. Only patrons with my taste will be permitted to dine here. You will personally visit me at my home at least once a month to make sure I am happy with your performance and to bring me specially prepared snacks. New dishes will be added regularly to the menu, to keep me from becoming bored, but they must please my discriminating palate. Also, you and your staff must never, *ever* offend or irritate me in any way."

The chef rubbed his chin thoughtfully. "But *monsieur*, if I did those things, the restaurant would go out of business. Surely it is enough to partake of good, wholesome nourishment in the company of others who also appreciate it."

A stormy look came over Arthur S. Nob's face. "Enough?" he cried, getting to his feet. "And you call yourself a *chef*? You obviously don't even know what a restaurant is all about!" Enraged, he slapped a few bills into the waiter's hand. "Keep the change," he muttered and strode out the door.

"Well," Arthur mumbled as he drove back to his new house to put a FOR SALE sign in the yard. "I knew there weren't any decent restaurants in this town."

Such a terrible burden to be a gourmet, he thought, shaking his head. But somebody had to do it. Chin high, he listened proudly as the growling in his stomach began once more.

14   The Christian Airplane🍃

Early one Saturday morning the phone rang. My friend Wilfred was on the line. "My project's finished!" he announced.

"What project?" I asked.

There was a pause, and his voice dropped to an intense whisper. "I've built a Christian airplane," he said.

"A what?"

"A Christian airplane," he repeated. "You've got to come see it. You know that little airfield north of town?"

"I think so," I said.

"Meet me there at noon. Boy, are you gonna be impressed!" With that he hung up.

I put the receiver down and scratched my chin. *A Christian airplane?* I thought. I'd never heard of such a thing. But Wilfred sounded as if he knew what he was talking about, so at a quarter to twelve I hopped into my car and headed for the airstrip.

When I got there, Wilfred grabbed me by the elbow and hurried me toward a nearby hangar. "It's around the corner," he said in that confident voice of his. "I built it in my garage, then towed it out here behind my station wagon."

"Really?" I asked. "Is that legal, to tow an airplane down the highway?"

He shrugged. "Who knows? But they wouldn't arrest me

for a little thing like that. After all, it's a *Christian* airplane—for a good cause."

I stopped. "Excuse me, Wilfred," I said. "What *is* a Christian airplane anyway? What's it for?"

"Why, for Christian stuff," he said impatiently. "Flying missionaries around, maybe even putting on Gospel stunt shows. C'mon, you've gotta see it." He grabbed my elbow again and led me around the corner of the hangar.

"There it is," he said proudly. "Pretty fantastic, don't you think?" I gazed in wonderment.

"Well?" he asked, impatient again.

"I—I don't know much about planes, Wilfred. But aren't they supposed to have wings?"

"Wings?" Wilfred asked, puzzled. "They would have been awfully expensive. I didn't exactly have a big budget, you know."

"Oh," I said. I studied the fuselage. "What's it made of?" I asked.

"Empty cereal boxes," he answered, smiling. "My nephew works in a supermarket, and he gave me all their damaged ones. Took me six months to collect enough of them."

"Very thrifty," I murmured. Bending over, I studied the cockpit.

"How do you like those controls? Great, huh?"

I peered at the panel, which had a Cheerios-box background, and saw an impressive array of dials and switches. There were a couple of alarm clocks, an old Mickey Mouse watch, a ruler, a Boy Scout compass, a radio dial, and a broken pocket calculator. Smack in the middle was a row of wall switches.

"What do the switches do?" I asked.

"Nothing," he said.

"Oh." I walked around the front of the plane. "This must be the propeller," I commented.

Joan 'n' the Whale

"Right," he answered. "Naturally, those real propellers cost a small fortune. So I used this agitating thing from my sister's old washing machine. Looks a lot like a prop, doesn't it?"

"Sure does," I said. "An amazing resemblance."

"Want to see the engine?" Wilfred asked. He opened a cardboard door on the side of the fuselage. "Look at that baby," he said proudly. "It ran my lawn mower perfectly for fifteen years. Now it's gonna power this plane."

I cocked my head to one side, doubtful. "A *lawn-mower* engine?" I asked. "Are you sure that's enough for an *airplane?*"

He waved my question aside and chuckled. "C'mon, man," he said. "This is a *Christian* airplane. The Lord knows we can't afford one of those fancy aircraft engines. Just as long as we're trusting him, what does it matter?"

"I . . . I guess you're right," I agreed sheepishly.

"Hey, it's all right." He spoke soothingly. "Even *my* faith used to flag once in a while. Now take a look at this." He pointed underneath the plane, where the landing gear would have been on a non-Christian aircraft.

"Very nice," I said. *"Two* pairs of roller skates, huh?"

"That extra margin of safety," Wilfred explained knowingly.

"Good idea," I approved.

"Now for the crowning touch," he declared, leading me to the rear of the plane. "Here's the most important part of the whole aircraft."

"The tail?" I asked.

"Nope."

"The fuel tank?"

"No," he answered with a laugh. "Take a look."

I did and saw a large fish symbol painted on the tail. "Oh," I said. "A Christian sign."

"Right," he gleefully exclaimed. "And John 3:16 is on the other side."

We stood there admiring the Christian airplane for a few moments before Wilfred spoke up again, excited. "Well, shall we go up?"

"Huh?" I said.

"I wanted to share the honor of the first flight with you, since you're such a good friend."

I swallowed. "You mean *fly* in it? I didn't know you knew how to fly, Wilfred."

"Ah, there can't be much to it. I've seen planes take off before. I even rode in one once." He climbed confidently into the cockpit.

"Uh . . . I'm not sure that's enough," I ventured nervously. "Aren't you supposed to take flying lessons, get a pilot's license?"

He laughed. "Oh, you of little faith," he said. "What do we need that stuff for? We're *Christians*. Nobody expects us to be professionals, after all."

"Uh—right. But there's only one chair. I guess you'll have to go up alone."

"You're right. I knew I'd forgotten something. Well, maybe next time." He reached between his feet, yanked the cord of the lawn-mower engine, and the motor putt-putted to life.

"Have you got a parachute?" I asked.

"Of course not," he said. "How could a *Christian* plane fail? Give me a push, will you?"

Gently, so as not to damage the cardboard, I pushed the plane a few feet. Soon it began to move under its own power, rolling along with the speed and sound of a go-cart.

"Up we go!" Wilfred cried, but the Christian airplane just buzzed along slowly on the ground until it crashed into the side of the control tower. Maybe *crumpled* would be a better word, as the cereal boxes just sort of collapsed without much noise.

I ran over to Wilfred. "Are you okay?"

"Of course," he called out, looking dazed.

"Too bad it was a flop," I said, shaking my head.

Wilfred looked sternly at me. "What are you *talking* about?" he demanded. "This is a *Christian* airplane. Just because it seems to us to have been unsuccessful doesn't mean a thing."

"Oh," I said.

"We planted a seed here today. Why, someone probably saw the fish sign on the tail and started thinking."

"You're right, Wilfred," I conceded, feeling ashamed of myself. "Here, let me help you clean up this mess."

"*Mess?*" he said indignantly. "We're going to leave this right here, as a witness."

After making sure the tail was sticking up out of the rubble, Wilfred walked back to the car with me. "Don't worry," he comforted me, putting an arm around my shoulder. "Someday this will all come together, and we'll see how it fits perfectly into God's plan. 'Til then, have faith."

He was right, of course. After all, he's been working on projects like the Christian airplane for years now. If *anybody* has faith after all that time, it's Wilfred.

And me, of course. . . . I think.

15

Waiting for the Ambulance

There had been an accident. It was the middle of the night, two dozen miles from anywhere.

The two cars sat crumpled like candy wrappers at the side of the road. Five people lay by the highway in various states of disrepair. They were all alive.

But they all needed the ambulance.

Fortunately, there was a pay phone about a hundred yards down the highway. One man, the youngest, limped the distance painfully, placed a call to the nearest town, and limped back to wait with the others.

"It's okay," he told them, breathing hard. "I talked to the ambulance driver. He'll be out to get us very soon."

"Thank heaven," sighed a woman who lay by the bushes, where she had been thrown. "This road is so deserted. I doubt anyone would have passed us until morning."

There was a long pause. They all listened, but heard only the sound of their breathing and an occasional cricket. Finally, from across the road, a large man in a business suit spoke.

"How do you know he's coming?" he asked gruffly. "I don't believe he is."

"He *promised* he would," the young man answered. "I talked to him myself."

"Hmph," the businessman said doubtfully.

Nearby, two elderly brothers, sporting identical white beards and perpetual scowls, leaned back to back against a speed-limit sign.

"Tell me, young man," said one. "Exactly what did the ambulance driver say?"

"Yes," added the other, "we must know his *exact* words."

The young man thought. "He said, 'Stay off the road and keep alert. Don't let anyone doze off. I'm about thirty-one miles away. I promise I'll be there just as soon as I can.' And that was it."

"Hmmm," one of the brothers said. Wincing, he managed to pull a pocket calculator out of his jacket. "Thirty-one miles. Let's see. . . . Average speed, fifty-five. . . . I figure he will arrive in exactly thirty-four minutes and twenty-four seconds."

The other brother took out his own calculator. "You're wrong, as usual. It's thirty-three minutes and forty-eight seconds."

"Balderdash!" shouted the first. "You're not allowing for the hundred yards between the phone booth and our present position."

"I am so!" retorted the second.

"Gentlemen, please," the young man said. "The ambulance driver didn't say *when* he would get here, only that he *would*. That's the important thing, isn't it?"

The brothers lowered their voices, but kept on arguing.

"Oh, my," said the woman, sounding worried. "Thirty-three or thirty-four minutes—how am I ever going to mend this dress before he gets here?" Struggling with a sprained elbow, she found a little sewing kit in her purse. "Owww," she moaned. "I've got so many things to do. I hope he doesn't get here *too* soon."

"He won't get here at *all*," growled the businessman. "I can't wait here forever. I'm going to get help myself."

The man proceeded to drag himself to his feet, then staggered in the opposite direction from the phone booth.

"Wait!" called the young man. "He'll be here. I know it."

"Ha!" said the businessman.

"But you're going the wrong way," persisted the young man.

The businessman's voice was fading. "There's bound to be a town in either direction," he declared. "I can take care of myself, boy." Then he was gone.

"I *have* it," cried one of the elderly brothers. " 'Stay off the road,' that ambulance man said. There's a hidden meaning there, if you study it closely. It means the ambulance will not arrive on the road at all, but out there in the trees and brush somewhere."

"No, in the hills," the other brother countered. "In any case, we must get away from the road immediately." Slowly they got up.

"Wait!" the young man said. "He didn't mean we were to leave the road!"

The brothers shook their heads. "Son, you have not studied the driver's statement as we have. There are mysteries here you cannot comprehend." They turned and wandered off into the night. For a while the young man could hear them arguing about whether they would hear the ambulance siren or see the flashing light first. Then he could hear them no more.

The young man shivered. "Are you still there?" he called to the woman.

"Yes, yes," she snapped. "But I'm very busy—ouch—I've got a million things to do before he gets here, and I don't want to be disturbed."

In a minute the young man felt himself starting to doze off. He shook himself. "Got to stay awake," he said. "Got to keep alert." Folding his arms against the cold, he stared into the darkness, wide-eyed.

The first pink hints of dawn were appearing in the sky by the time they heard the siren. The distant wail made the young man smile.

"Oh, no, no!" cried the woman, looking up from the dress she was still mending. "He can't come *yet*. I've still got so much to do!"

She looked around, frantic. "I've got to hide," she said. "He can come back and get me later. I've just *got* to finish this dress."

Gathering up her sewing kit, she stumbled awkwardly off the shoulder and into the trees. "Don't let him find me!" she pleaded. "I'm not ready yet!" She disappeared into the woods, leaving the young man sitting all by himself.

He struggled to stand as the ambulance, red lights flashing, screeched to a halt in front of him.

"What happened to the others?" the driver asked, surveying the scene.

"They left," the young man answered. "They didn't believe or weren't ready or got too involved in something else."

The driver nodded. "That happens," he said and helped the young man into the back of the vehicle.

Inside, the young man lay down on the cot and breathed a thankful sigh. He was safe at last. Then he looked around, surprised.

"Say," he called out to the driver. "This is a pretty small ambulance, isn't it? I mean, you couldn't get a whole lot of people in it."

"That's true," the driver replied. "But," he added with a sad note in his voice, "there weren't a whole lot of people left waiting for me, were there?"

16 How I Sold My Vacuum Cleaner 🍃

I was feeling lower than a snake's navel. I mean, I'd been going to the Main Street Vacuum Cleaner Store almost every Sunday since I was born. I'd become a vacuum cleaner salesman when I was just six or seven. But even now I'd never sold a vacuum cleaner in my life!

The head salesman at the store didn't make things any easier. Every week he reminded us that we were supposed to be out there selling vacuums. "Personally owning a vacuum cleaner is the most important thing in the world!" he'd say, and we'd all nod our heads. But when it came right down to it, I couldn't admit to anybody outside the store that I even *owned* a vacuum.

I told myself I could be a "silent salesman." But that didn't work too well. One day I was in my living room, changing the bag on my vacuum cleaner, when the doorbell rang. Without even waiting for me to open the door, Mrs. Zumbrowski, from down the street, barged in.

"Hi, there!" she said. I almost jumped out of my skin.

"What vacuum?" I cried, trying to hide it. "I don't know what you're talking about!"

She looked at me sideways and cocked an eyebrow. "Say," she said, "I've been noticing something different about you. You've got something the rest of us on this street don't have. What is it, anyway?"

I gulped. "Uh, my curtains?" I asked, trying to stuff the vacuum cleaner into the closet. "They're made of . . . cloth. Unusual."

"No, that's not it," she said, frowning. Then it hit her. "*I* know! You've got a vacuum cleaner, haven't you?"

"Never heard of it," I croaked, attempting to wrap myself around the machine. "You must have me mixed up with somebody else."

"But isn't *that* a vacuum cleaner?" she asked, pointing at it.

I panicked. "Oh, that? No, that's . . . uh . . . my *dog!* Yeah, that's right!" I patted the machine's handle. "Good Fido. Good boy."

She looked at me as though I'd decided to wear my shoes on my head. "Hmmm," she said, backing away. "Sure *looked* like a vacuum cleaner." Staring blankly, I kept patting the dust bag until she disappeared down the sidewalk.

Finally I collapsed, feeling worse than ever. Was it any wonder my friends didn't want to buy a vacuum cleaner from me?

But I couldn't give up, not with our head salesman reminding us each week of our responsibility. So I decided to watch an older salesman at work. Mr. Gumbleton, who's been coming to the Main Street Vacuum Cleaner Store for forty or fifty years now, was glad to help me.

"You've got to pull out all the stops and be aggressive," he said, carrying his soapbox to the corner of Main and Broadway. "That's the only approach these people respect." He mounted his soapbox, rolled up his sleeves, and fired away.

"You pigs!" he yelled, wagging his finger in the general direction of the passersby. "Your floors are filthy! Your carpets are a disgrace! You should be ashamed of yourselves!" People just stared.

"Woe to you who have not vacuum cleaners!" he bellowed. "Your houses will be engulfed in dirt! Your brooms are powerless! You must buy a vacuum, and you must buy it now!"

By then a small crowd had gathered to watch. But when Mr. Gumbleton finished, they all drifted away, shaking their heads and snickering.

Mr. Gumbleton didn't seem disturbed. "A wonderful day of selling today!" he told me cheerily, stepping down from his soapbox. "You see, these people have been so struck with their need for vacuum cleaners that they've all run home to get their money!"

We stood there waiting for the people to come back and buy, but after three or four hours I had to leave. "Uh, thanks," I told Mr. Gumbleton.

"Don't mention it," he said to no one in particular.

Boy, I thought. *I'll never sell any vacuum cleaners that way.*

Then I got an idea. *What I need is an instruction book!* So the next day I picked up a pamphlet called "Vacuum Cleaner Salesmanship" at the store, grabbed my vacuum, and nervously headed across the street.

A lady in a bathrobe answered my first knock. "Yes?" she said.

"Good day, Mrs. Insert Name Here," I read from the book as fast as I could, without looking up. "I'm from the Main Street Vacuum Cleaner Store, and I'd like to tell you the features of our MSV-17 cleaner. The armature is connected to the seventh screw of the plate containing the brush housing; under the suction fastener is the tube connector, black Bakelite and adjustable to a forty-five-degree angle."

"What?" she cried. With a disgusted snort she slammed the door.

Must be in a bad mood, I thought. So I tried the next house, where an old man in a T-shirt and Bermuda shorts opened the door.

"Good day, Mr. Insert Name Here," I read. "I'm from the Main Street Vacuum Cleaner Store, and I'd like to. . . ." I got halfway through my pitch when the old man said something about how that sounded good, that he could really use a vacuum cleaner. But I wasn't about to let my presentation be interrupted again.

"... The 2.5 horsepower, AC-120 motor with prelubricated bearings is served by a spring-activated switch with a U-joint pivot. Wouldn't you like to own this excellent machine?" But when I finally looked up, the door was closed. I couldn't figure out why.

Dejected, I went home and switched on the TV. A famous vacuum cleaner salesman in a sparkly white suit was on channel 13. His name was Brother Dusty, and his show was called "The Upright Hour." *Hey,* I thought, *maybe, if I watch this, I can pick up some selling tips.*

I watched, but for some reason Brother Dusty never got around to selling any vacuum cleaners. He had plenty of commercials for Brother Dusty bumper stickers, charm bracelets, autographed photos, and a guided tour of the ancient factory where vacuum cleaners were first made. But that was about it.

With a sigh I switched off the TV. *How am I ever going to learn how to sell vacuum cleaners?* I thought. *I've tried silence, shouting, going door to door. . . . What's left?*

I thought back to last Sunday's meeting at the vacuum cleaner store. Our head salesman had told us to "go out to the highways and byways and bring them in." *That's it!* I thought excitedly. *All I have to do is get people to come to the store, and the head salesman will do the rest! How simple can you get?*

Next day I ran into my friend Bob Berkleman at the supermarket. *Here goes,* I thought.

"Uh, hi, Bob," I began. "How are you?"

"Fine," he answered, picking out a head of lettuce. I sort of hid my vacuum behind the tomato display.

"Say, Bob," I said, "I'd like to invite you to come to the vacuum cleaner store with me next week."

He dropped the lettuce into his cart and stared at me. "The *vacuum cleaner store?*" he groaned in disbelief. "Why would I want to go *there?*"

I swallowed. "Uh, I can't tell you."

"Why not?"

I was starting to sweat. "Look, you'll really enjoy it," I said. "We've got a great head salesman; he gives a great sales talk—"

"Hey, wait a minute," Bob said suspiciously, peering over the tomatoes. "Haven't *you* got a vacuum cleaner?"

"Well, uh, yes," I mumbled.

"Then why don't *you* try to sell me on it? Doesn't yours work?"

I blushed. "It—it's not that. It's just that . . . I'm not a *professional* salesman. We have people who are *trained* to do that sort of thing."

Bob shook his head. "No way, man. My mother used to take me to the vacuum cleaner store when I was a kid. I was bored stiff!"

I tried to tell him that he wouldn't be bored, that we were having a movie about vacuums and a special speaker ɔm company headquarters—but he was already gone. *I'm a failure,* I thought, leaning on my vacuum and staring at the floor. *I'll never be any good as a salesman.*

My sad gaze fell on a little pile of broken glass at my feet. Someone had dropped a jar of peanuts or something. *Janitor must have missed it,* I thought absently. *Might as well clean it up; don't want anybody to get hurt.* I found an outlet, plugged the cord of my vacuum into it, and went to work.

I was almost done when I heard a voice. I looked up and saw my neighbor Mrs. Zumbrowski, watching me intently. "Excuse me," she said, "but I couldn't help noticing your vacuum cleaner there. It seems to work really well."

I shrugged. "I guess it does, as a matter of fact," I said glumly.

"Really gets it clean, eh?" she asked, pointing at the floor.

I switched off the machine and rolled up the cord. "That's right," I said with a sigh.

"Do you suppose *I* could get one of those?" she asked.

I stared at her. *She—she's asking how she can get a vacuum cleaner?* I thought. My heart stopped. *What do I do now?*

When my heart finally started again, I stuttered, "I—I'd be glad to tell you how I got mine."

"Okay," she said matter-of-factly.

So I did.

That's how I sold my first vacuum cleaner. And that's how I learned that what the company really needs is ... more demonstration models.

17

The Last Division🌿

F rom the beginning, there was the war.

It was the Kingdom versus the Principalities. Everyone was loyal to one side or the other. But all agreed the Principalities had started the fight—and wouldn't stop until every square inch of the Kingdom was subjugated or scorched.

For what seemed like ages the Principalities advanced steadily, crushing freedom and installing tyranny everywhere. Fear reigned. But one day the tide turned when a young general from Kingdom Headquarters burst onto the scene. At great personal risk, he charged deep into enemy territory.

The general's bold act did not end the war, but galvanized his people to fight again. Thousands volunteered; almost overnight the Kingdom Army mushroomed from a dozen clumsy recruits into a fully manned fighting machine. Stunned, the Principalities lost ground daily.

Within days of his victory, however, the general had to leave. Headquarters had called him home. After bidding farewell to his handpicked lieutenants, he departed—leaving behind two of his few possessions. One was a two-way radio; the other, an army procedure manual for the instruction of the men.

Both were put to good use during the next few years.

Every good Kingdom soldier carried a manual in his pack, consulting its rules and diagrams faithfully. Each day the general's orders and words of comfort were heard over the radio. And the Kingdom continued to gain ground.

But when the original lieutenants passed from the scene, things changed. New officers were promoted; memories of the general grew faint. Soon the radio and the manual were consulted less and less often, and the advance of the Kingdom began to slow.

Finally the Kingdom's progress reached a standstill. Fighting at the front was as fierce as ever, but neither side could gain anything but casualties. So serious was the crisis that one murky evening the Kingdom's field officers met in a bunker to take drastic action.

An elderly colonel spoke first. "The problem is that the general isn't here anymore. Why, my grandfather used to say that a mere handful of men could take an enemy fortress after a few words from the general."

A young major's reply was icy. "The general won't help us now," he said. "Nobody's heard from him—or headquarters—for years. Anyway, we can't rely on a single general when we have so many talented officers ready to lead."

"Absolutely," agreed a captain, polishing a medal on his own chest.

"Let's divide our forces into groups," the major continued. "We could have an airborne division, an infantry division, an armored division, an amphibious division, a missile division—"

"Now, wait a minute," the old colonel said with a frown. "We can't make such a sweeping change without consulting the manual. What does the book have to say about this?"

"Nothing," the major replied with a yawn. "There weren't any divisions in the general's day. Things were primitive then."

"Hmmmph," said the colonel, fumbling in his pack for a

Joan 'n' the Whale

copy of the manual. But he couldn't find one, and neither could anyone else. Someone suggested trying to raise headquarters on the radio, but everyone agreed that the batteries were probably dead.

The colonel shrugged. Finally the major called for a vote: "Shall we divide our forces?" Slowly, one by one, the officers around the table said, "Aye."

And so the divisions were born.

The experiment was an immediate success. Within the month the Principalities reeled as the Kingdom's airborne division let loose a torrent of bombs. They scattered at the advance of the armored division; they retreated before the infantry, commando, and amphibious divisions; they cowered in the face of the missile and artillery divisions.

The Kingdom was on the march again. Slow but steady advances brought more and more of the Principalities under the benevolent influence of the Kingdom, and the power of the divisions grew with every new victory.

Years passed; as they did, fewer soldiers spoke of the army as a whole. One's division became the main object of allegiance.

It was then that the commander of the airborne division had an idea. "You know," he said one day, looking down at his green uniform, "I've never liked this color. I think we should wear purple instead."

"*Purple?*" echoed a captain.

"Affirmative," his superior replied. "Purple is such a royal color. And the airborne *is* a cut above those *other* divisions."

"And we don't need to blend in with jungle brush, like the infantry," the captain added. "We need a color befitting our higher status and tastes."

The order went out. Soon the airborne division was known throughout the Kingdom for its bright, new, purple uniforms.

But the color change shocked the infantry division. *"Purple uniforms?"* cried the field marshal of the infantry. "Don't those flying fools know their manuals? The book specifically requires that all soldiers wear green uniforms."

"S-sir," a corporal stammered, "exactly where does the manual say that?"

The head officer checked his pockets for the book, but couldn't find it. His face turned red. "Do you expect me to know the page number?" he roared. "I know it's in there somewhere. So from now on, the infantry will be greener than ever. I want every infantryman to wear green boots, green underwear—and green hair!"

"Green hair?" the corporal cried.

"Dye it!" his superior barked. "No one's going to get us mixed up with those purple pansies!"

"Yes, sir," the corporal said with a sigh.

The news of green-haired infantrymen was soon received with disgust at the armored division. "This is an abomination," muttered the chief officer. "The general would never have stood for this, I'm sure. Tell the men that from this day on every member of the armored division will shave his head. We'll separate ourselves from these renegade infantrymen, once and for all!" It was done as he ordered.

Meanwhile, the artillery division was furious. "What are those other divisions doing, playing games?" the artillery commander thundered. "Don't they know there's a war on?"

"We would never stoop to such foolishness," one of his aides said. "We read the manual every day; I hear the other divisions *never* do."

"That's right," the commander declared. "Starting now, we'll ship no more ammunition to divisions that fail to meet our standards. All communication with them will be cut off. If necessary, we'll fight this war entirely by ourselves!"

The break led to a chain reaction. The commando division halted contact with the artillery division, in sympathy with the infantry. The airborne, deprived of explosives, spread a rumor that the artillery was really spying for the Principalities. That led the missile division to break with artillery, as did amphibious and engineering.

Rumors flew faster and thicker. Before long no one was talking to anyone else.

Progress on all fronts stopped. Each division turned inward, trying to make its own weapons, grow its own food, and boost its own morale by emphasizing its "distinctives."

Airborne uniforms were tinted a deeper purple. The infantry grew mustaches and beards just so they could dye them green and promoted the men who had the greenest eyes. The armored division made failure to shave one's eyebrows a capital offense and prohibited the wearing of helmets so that bald heads could be more prominently displayed.

Artillery, meanwhile, declared itself "the one true division, faithful alone to the principles of the general." Its members prided themselves on their ability to quote whole chapters of the manual from memory. Deep in a lead-lined vault beneath their command post they hid their most prized treasure: the two-way radio left by the general himself, now corroded and silent.

It was only a matter of time before the inevitable occurred. No one was sure who fired the first shot; rumor had it that an artillery sniper mistook an infantryman for the enemy. Overnight the word spread that the battle of the divisions had begun. Forgetting the Principalities, the army of the Kingdom turned at last upon itself.

By now the planes and guns of the Kingdom had rusted. So the soldiers resorted to hand-to-hand combat, using fists and stones against their former comrades. The process was slow; there was far more maiming than killing.

Many years have passed since the war began. To this very day, the battle rages on.

But for as long as anyone can remember, the Principalities have not had to fire a single shot.

18

Hailing the Chief ✏

Here sat at his desk in the Oval Office, waiting. He waited, even though there was a stack of letters to sign, a cable to read, a press conference to prepare for, a briefing with the cabinet to attend, a tea for an ambassador in the Rose Garden. . . .

Looking up from his schedule, he smiled. Yes, there *was* a lot to do. But first some people were coming—some very important people.

At least *he* thought they were very important. That was why he kept inviting them to come to the Oval Office and talk with him. He longed to hear what was in their hearts and minds, to talk about how they felt, what they needed, how they could help him accomplish his goals. . . .

"Mr. President," said a voice on the intercom. "They're here, sir."

"Ah," he said. "Send the first one in, please." He leaned forward on the edge of his chair, waiting.

The door opened, and a housewife ushered herself into the room. Without acknowledging the president's smile or outstretched hand, she plopped down in a chair. Then she shut her eyes tight.

"Dear Mr. President," she said in a nasal, singsong voice. "Thank you for the world so sweet, thank you for the food we eat, thank you for the birds that sing, thank you, sir, for everything. Good-bye."

Before the president could say a word in response, the woman opened her eyes, got up, and walked out the door.

He sighed. Why did it always seem to go like this? He pushed the intercom button. "Next, please," he said.

The door opened, and in came a stout man who wore a tuxedo. Again the president's hand was ignored.

"O thou chief executive who art in the White House," said the man, clasping his hands and looking at the ceiling. "O thou in whom so much doth constitutionally dwell, upon whose desk hath been placed a most effective blotter; incline thine ear toward thy most humble citizen, and grant that thy many entities may be manifoldly endowed upon the fruitful plain. . . ."

Wincing, the president closed his eyes and rubbed his temples.

"And may thy thou dost harkeneth whatly didst shalt evermore in twain asunder," the man concluded in a loud monotone.

"Excuse me," said the president, "but what—"

"Good-bye," said the man, seeming not to hear, and walked out.

The president sighed again. "Next, please," he spoke into the intercom.

This time when the door opened, there seemed to be no one there. Then the president looked down and saw a man crawling through the doorway on his hands and knees.

"Oh, Mr. g-great and awful P-president," blubbered the man, not looking up from the carpet. "I am but a disgusting piece of filth in your presence. No, I am less than that! How dare I enter here? How dare I think that you would do anything but grind me into the floor?"

"Please, get up," said the president, offering his hand. "You don't have to do that. I *want* to talk with you."

But the man went right on groveling. "I deserve only to be squashed under the weight of your mighty desk," he whined. "I could never have gotten an invitation to talk with

Joan 'n' the Whale

you. It must have been a mistake. How can you ever forgive me for breaking in like this? Oh, I'm so sorry, so sorry, so sorry. . . ." Still on his hands and knees, he crawled out.

The man's groaning faded down the hall. The president shook his head, then slowly pushed the intercom button. "Next," he said, sounding tired.

In moments a young man entered. He was wearing headphones and bobbing up and down to the music of his pocket stereo.

"Hey, prez," the young man said, ignoring the offered hand. "What's happening?" He looked out the window. "Nice place you've got here. I'm, like, *so* glad we could have this little chat, you know? You're not bad for an old dude, I guess. You don't bother me, I won't bother you, okay? Well, I've gotta go. Hang in there." He walked out.

The president drummed his fingers on his desk. "Next, please," he said wearily.

An elderly man marched in, staring at a piece of paper in his hand. He, too, ignored the president's greeting. "Mr. President," he declared, keeping his eyes on his list, "I want there to be a parking space waiting for me when I go downtown this afternoon. Not a parallel parking space, either— one I can drive right into. Not one with a parking meter. You can see to it that none of those meter maids gives me a ticket. Now, this is important!"

The president cleared his throat politely. "Speaking of important," he ventured, "how do you feel about my program to feed the hungry? Would you like to have a part in—"

"And another thing!" the man continued. "I lost my best golf club. A putter. Can't remember where I put it. Now, you find it for me, will you? Got to have that club before Saturday. I know you can do it. Good-bye."

With that the old man got up and shuffled out the door.

The president slumped in his chair. "Next," he said.

There was a pause. At last a young woman entered

slowly. She looked like a sleepwalker—eyes nearly shut, jaw slack, her feet dragging. She yawned and slid into a chair. "Dear . . . Mr . . . President . . . ," she said, her head drooping. "I know I should talk to you when I'm more . . . awake . . . but I've got so many things to do. . . . So . . . sleepy. . . . There was something I was going to say. . . . What . . . is . . . ? I was going to say . . . uh. . . ." She started to snore.

The president buzzed his secretary, who stepped in. "Could you help this young lady out?" he asked, sighing again.

"Certainly, Mr. President," said the secretary and helped the dozing girl to her feet.

The president gazed sadly out the window. "How many do we have left?" he asked.

"I'm sorry, sir," the secretary said. "But as usual, most of the people you sent invitations to said they were too busy to talk. They had to watch TV, wax the car, do the dishes. . . ."

"Oh," said the president, dejected. "Isn't there *anyone* out there?"

"There is *one*, sir," she said. "But you wouldn't want to talk with him."

"Why not?"

"Because he's—just a *child*, Mr. President."

The chief executive shrugged. "May as well show him in," he said.

Moments later a little boy entered shyly. He looked around the room, his eyes wide. "Are—are you really the *president?*" he asked.

The president smiled. "I really am," he answered, offering his hand.

The little boy reached up and shook it. Then he sat down, folded his hands in his lap, and waited.

The president watched, amazed, as the boy sat politely for nearly a minute. "Isn't there . . . something you want to

tell me?" the president asked finally. "Something you have to recite, or ask for, or say?"

The little boy looked down for a moment, thinking. Then he looked up. "Yes," he said. "I guess there is."

"Well, what is it?" the president asked.

"Thank you for inviting me," the boy said. "That's all."

When the president heard that, he couldn't seem to say anything for a while. All he could do was smile.

But then they talked and talked and talked for the longest, most wonderful time.

19

Casey
at the Pulpit✒

T he outlook wasn't brilliant at the Mudville Church that day;
Pastor Casey, who was worried, took one minute more to pray.
He knew that if his sermon seemed to quaver, drag, or lurch,
A sickly silence soon would fall upon First Mudville Church.

A restless few got up to go before his start. The rest
Sat in their pews like corpses, which was what they did the best.
They thought, *If only Casey were the* entertaining *type,*
We'd even put up money then; we'd like a little hype.

For some exceeded Casey, in their style and in their dress,
Those TV preachers, singing groups, comedians, and the rest;
So upon that drowsy multitude grim melancholy sat,
For there seemed but little chance of trading Casey in for that.

Then during the announcements, to the wonderment of all,
The pastor told a joke and sent a giggle through the hall;
But when the dust had lifted, and they saw what had occurred,
He was taking out his Bible; he was about to teach the Word!

So from a hundred throats or more there rose a lusty yawn;
It rumbled through the sanctuary, rattled on the lawn;
It knocked upon the steeple and recoiled upon the beach,
For Casey, Pastor Casey, would soon begin to preach.

There was hope in Casey's manner as he stepped into his place;
There were notes on Casey's pulpit and a smile on Casey's face.
And when, responding to the yawns, he looked up at the clock,
Each stranger in the crowd could hear each little tick and tock.

Two hundred eyes were closing as he opened up the book;
A hundred heads were nodding, planning Sunday roasts to cook.
And while the congregation held their hymnbooks in their laps,
They settled down to take their very long and spiritual naps.

And now the opening Bible truth came hurtling through the air;
The members sat a-watching it in haughty grandeur there.
Close by the sleepy churchmen the truth unheeded sped—
"That ain't our style," they mumbled. "Point one," the pastor said.

From the benches, black with people, there went up a muffled
    snore,
Like the whirring of a buzz saw on a stern and distant shore.
"Fire him! Fire the preacher!" muttered someone in the pews;
But they'd fired so many already, there was no one left to choose.

With a smile of Christian charity poor Casey's visage shone;
Despite the deadly stillness, he pushed the sermon on;
He looked down at his outline, and once more the insights flew;
But the people still ignored it—even though he said, "Point two."

"ZZZZZZZ," snored the congregation, and the echo answered,
    "ZZZZZZZ." But
One loud "Amen!" from Casey, and the audience went, "What?"
They saw his face grow stern and cold; they saw his muscles
    strain,
And they knew he wouldn't let them let that truth go by again.

The smile is gone from Casey's lip; his notes are clenched in hand;
He pounds with great intensity his fist upon the stand.
And now he starts to make his point, and now he lets it flow,
And afterward the people tell him, "Pastor, way to go!"

Oh, somewhere in this favored land the Son is shining bright;
The organ's playing somewhere, and somewhere hearts are light;
And somewhere folks are learning, and somewhere Christians
    shout;
But there is no growth in Mudville—Pastor Casey's been tuned
    out.

20 The Man Who Built His House Upon a Rock

Behold, there was a man who built his house upon a rock.

When he had finished building his house upon a rock, he laughed, saying, "Oh, how wise I am to build my house upon a rock! And how foolish is the man next door who built his house upon the sand! For it is written that when the rain descends, and the floods come, and the winds blow, and beat upon these houses, the one founded upon the rock will fall not. But great will be the fall of the house built upon the sand. Oh, ha-ha-ha!"

So laughing, the man who built his house upon a rock went into his house and locked the door. "Now I will relax and wait for the storm warnings," he said, "for my house is founded safe upon a rock."

He did wait. And he waited and waited.

Nothing happened.

There was no rain, no flood, no wind—not even a mild drizzle.

"Hey, wait a minute," said the man who built his house upon a rock. "There's supposed to be a big storm, and the house built upon the sand is supposed to fall down. *Everybody* knows *that.*"

So he watched the sky, hoping for a hurricane or at least a major hailstorm; but there was nothing.

"Well," said the man, perplexed. "I'm sure that storm will come along any minute now. In the meantime, that man who built his house upon the sand must be pretty nervous. I'll bet he's having a *terrible* time in that flimsy little house of his!"

Chuckling smugly, he looked over at the house built upon the sand. He expected to see his neighbor pacing anxiously back and forth, worried about a storm. But the neighbor was smiling and laughing, making sand castles with friends in front of his house. They all seemed to be having a wonderful time.

"This is outrageous!" said the man who had built his house upon a rock. "Those people should be miserable, not happy. They should be begging for shelter in *my* house, hoping to escape the rain and the floods and the wind!"

He continued to listen to the weather reports, waiting for the storm to arrive; but still the skies remained clear.

One day, however, the man heard noises from next door. They were the noises of pounding and yelling. "Aha!" he said. "At last the storm has come, and my neighbor's house upon the sand is falling! How great will be the fall of it!"

But when he rushed to the window, he discovered that his neighbor was turning the house upon the sand into a luxury beachfront resort. The neighbor was grinning from ear to ear, wearing an expensive suit, studying blueprints, and directing work crews. Soon a fancy car drove up, and a beautiful woman dressed in a mink coat got out and gave the neighbor a kiss.

"Where is that storm?" bellowed the man who had built his house upon a rock. "The *wise* man builds his house upon the rock, the *foolish* man builds his house upon the sand, and the rains come tumbling *down! Everybody* knows *that!"*

Behold, the rains *did* come tumbling down. But they tumbled only on the house that had been built upon a rock. Not a drop fell on the house that had been built upon the sand.

"Why *me?"* moaned the man who had built his house

upon a rock. "My house may stand firm, but I have to patch the roof, clean the gutters, and bail out the basement. What must my neighbor do? Nothing!"

So it was in the months and years that followed. The man who built his house upon the sand got richer and richer, more and more successful, happier and happier. The man who built his house upon a rock patched the roof, cleaned the gutters, and bailed out the basement.

Finally, years and years after he had built his house upon a rock, the man threw up his hands. "I give up!" he said. "I've waited and waited, watched the sky, patched and cleaned and bailed. A record rainfall has descended on my house, and there's never been so much as a mist on my neighbor's. Any fool can see that there's not going to *be* any storm." With that he packed his suitcase and went next door to the luxury beachfront resort built upon the sand. "If you can't beat 'em, join 'em," he said.

That night, of course, the rain descended, and the floods came, and the winds blew and beat upon both those houses. The one that was built upon the sand fell; and great was the fall of it.

The other one fell not; for it was founded upon a rock.

Too bad nobody was home.

21

A Pocketful
of Change

Once upon a time there was a man who had a pocketful of change.

It wasn't a *big* pocketful, but the man thought it was enough. After all, hadn't he chosen each coin long ago? Hadn't he paid dearly for each one? Now he could use them to accomplish his purposes.

Or so he thought.

"Let's see," he said, reaching into his pocket. "How much have I got here?" He counted the coins into his palm. "One nickel, three dimes, a penny, two quarters, a fifty-cent piece, and a silver dollar." He smiled. "Good! Now I can use them to buy the things I need."

So off he went down the street, whistling happily. He whistled so loudly, in fact, that he couldn't hear the tiny, tinny racket that was coming from his pocket.

"I don't like it in here," the fifty-cent piece was saying. "It's too crowded and stuffy. And I don't like having to associate with coins of lower denominations."

"Look who's talking," said the silver dollar. "I'm worth twice your value. You're just overweight."

One of the quarters scoffed. "You're both out of date," he said. "You're useless in today's vending-machine world. People much prefer our slim, sleek shapes. Why don't you go back to the mint, where you came from?"

The dollar glared. "Well, at least we're not *dimes*. They're the smallest coins of all and the easiest to lose. Not that they'd be missed, mind you."

"Size isn't everything!" said the dimes in chorus. "Each of us is worth *twice* as much as that chubby nickel."

"*Well*," the nickel said, indignant. "You're forgetting the lowliest coin of all. I'm glad I'm not a *penny*. A penny can't buy *anything* anymore!"

The penny, who couldn't think of anything clever to say, blushed a coppery red. All the other coins laughed at him.

Finally the penny sighed. "I guess you're right," he said. "I don't know why the man bothers to carry me around in this pocket. I'm worthless to him. He could never use *me* to buy anything he needed." The others noisily agreed, clinking and snickering and saying that he wasn't worth a plugged nickel.

Meanwhile, the man had whistled and walked so far that he was getting hungry. Soon he came to a vending machine that sold candy bars.

"I *am* getting hungry," he said, "and those candy bars do look good. I think I'll use my two quarters to get a snack." With that he reached into his pocket.

"Oh, no, you don't!" the quarters said, too faintly for the man to hear. They burrowed deeper into the pocket. "No one's going to take *us* out of our nice, warm home. We'll hide down here until that hand goes away. Let the man use some *other* coin."

But no other coin would fit the man's purpose. So he dug deeper—and the deeper he dug, the deeper the quarters burrowed. Before long, the quarters found a little hole in the bottom of the man's pocket.

"Aha!" the quarters cried. "Here's our chance to escape. Now we can get away from the man and spend our lives as we please!" Pushing with all their might, the quarters forced their way through the little hole.

Joan 'n' the Whale

"We're free!" they cried, falling unnoticed to the sidewalk. "We can go anywhere, do anything we want!" But they found themselves rolling out of control, spinning into the gutter. With a *splish* they hit the dirty water and lay helpless, their shiny faces pointed at the sky.

The man sighed, pulling his hand from his pocket. "I thought I had two quarters," he said. "But I guess not." Still hungry, he continued down the street.

In the pocket, one of the dimes was getting an idea. "Hey," he said. "I'm tired of always being put down because of my size. I've never liked being a dime anyway. Let's turn ourselves into *quarters!*"

"Yeah!" said the other two dimes. "Quarters get a lot more attention. Since those two left, the man is bound to need some more. Won't *he* be impressed with how important we are!"

So the dimes gathered all their strength. They puffed themselves up, trying to look like quarters.

Just then the man came to a telephone booth. "I've got to make a call," he said. "And those three dimes in my pocket will help me do it."

He dug into his pocket and pulled out the dimes, who were still puffing themselves up, holding their breaths, pretending to be quarters. But they still looked like dimes. "Ah," the man said, "there you are. I'll just put the three of you into this pay phone so I can make that important call."

"*What?*" the dimes cried to each other in their tiny voices. "Why, we've never been so insulted! Can't he see that our true calling is to be quarters? Who does he think he is, anyway, restricting our self-worth?" With that they wriggled from the man's fingers and fell to the sidewalk.

"We'll find someone who appreciates our *real* value," the dimes sniffed. But like the quarters, they rolled into the gutter where the man couldn't find them.

"My, my," the man said, sighing again. "None of the

other coins is useful to me in making this phone call. I guess I'll have to go into a store and get change for my fifty-cent piece." So he entered the next store on the street.

"Whoa!" the fifty-cent piece growled from deep in the man's pocket. "He's not going to exchange *me* for inferior coins. I hate lying in a dark cash register drawer with all those strangers. I'm a big, important coin, and I want to stay that way!" Grunting and squeezing, the fifty-cent piece worked his way through the little hole in the man's pocket and fell to the floor. There he rolled under a counter, lost in the dust.

"Help," he cried weakly. But no one could hear.

The man rummaged in his pocket. "I was *sure* I had a fifty-cent piece," he told the cashier. "But I guess not." He thought for a moment. "Maybe I could use my silver dollar to get change. I'll just get twice as much, that's all."

The dollar roared a miniature roar. "Never!" he said. "I'm not going to be anybody's second choice. I'm the most valuable coin there is! I should be kept safe in the bank, not left to tarnish in this dump!" Harrumphing, the dollar coin slipped through the hole in the pocket and tried to leap onto the counter. But he fell short, plunging into a nearby trash can. There he blustered and fumed—but couldn't budge.

"I guess I don't have a silver dollar after all," the man said sadly, finding none in his pocket. Apologizing to the clerk, he left the store.

The man walked and walked and walked. Finally he reached the spot where he'd parked his car. There he saw a meter maid putting a parking ticket on his windshield.

"Wait," the man cried. "I have a nickel I can put in the parking meter. I'll just get it out of my pocket—"

"No way!" the nickel protested. "You're not spending *me* on some parking meter. I have higher ambitions. I want to help build a great big hospital or buy a fancy new yacht!"

The nickel jumped through the hole—only to fall under a car's muddy tire, stuck.

"I guess I don't have that nickel either," the man said, shaking his head. The meter maid handed him the parking ticket and drove away.

The man sighed once more. "Well," he said. "I thought I had a whole pocketful of change to use. But all I've got now is no candy bar, no phone call, a parking ticket, and no money. Except, that is, for this little penny."

The penny, who had been clinging desperately to the man's pocket so as not to slip through the hole in the bottom, sighed with relief as the man's fingers took hold of him. "Oh, use *me!*" the penny cried. "Maybe you could use me to buy a gum ball. I'm afraid I'm not good for much else."

The man brought the penny close to his eyes. "Hmm," he said, looking and frowning. Then he turned the penny over. "Aha!" he exclaimed, his frown turning to a smile. Holding the penny firmly in his hand, he whistled and walked down the street. The penny, unable to see or hear, waited breathlessly to find out whether the man could find a way to use him.

Finally the man stopped walking. Moments later the penny could see and hear again—and discovered he was lying on a counter in a store. It was a very nice store. Looking up, the penny saw a sign on the wall.

RARE COINS BOUGHT AND SOLD, the sign said.

"That's a valuable penny, all right," a kind-looking lady behind the counter was saying to the man. "A 1909-S VDB. It's worth about two hundred dollars!"

The penny gasped. "I—I am?" he asked. "I *am?*"

So it happened that the man, who knew a great deal about coins, sold the little penny for quite a bit of money. The penny, who was happy as could be, was displayed in a place of honor—in an elegant glass case—and the man had enough money to get all the candy bars and phone calls he could want and pay his parking ticket, too.

The other coins? They just sat in their gutters and dust, wondering why no one ever used them anymore.

"No one recognizes how *valuable* we are," they said crossly. "After all, we're not a bunch of *pennies* or something!"

They lived unhappily ever after.

22

The Facts🌿

T his . . . is the city.

Jerusalem, Judea.

A lot of people live here. A lot of people die here. But nobody lives here, dies here, and then lives again here.

Nobody.

I carry a badge. It's my job to make sure the decent people in this town don't get misled by a lot of religious fanatics. You know the type. Spreading rumors—rumors about people rising from the dead.

My name's Saturday. My partner's Bill Sunday.

Monday, April 7, 10:20 A.M. We were at headquarters, making out reports on a small-time hood named Barabbas. The captain walked up. "Okay, boys," he barked. "We've got another one."

"Resurrection rumor?" I said.

"Right," he said. "The chief wants you to drop whatever you're doing and look into it. He wants you to get—"

"The facts?" I said.

"Right." He gave us the details. A rabbi had been killed the previous Friday.

"Murder, eh?" Sunday theorized.

The captain shook his head. "Execution. Criminal.

Claimed to be a king. Now the body's missing. Rumor is he's alive again."

"That's a 512," I said. "Theft and concealment of a body with intent to perpetuate a rumor about a resurrected rabbi."

The captain nodded. "The chief wants you to go the whole nine furlongs on this one, boys. Rumors are flying, and he wants them stopped."

"We'll do our best, captain," I promised.

"I know I can count on you, boys." He paused. "That's because you always get—"

"The facts?" I said.

"Right," he said.

Monday, April 7, 11:03 A.M. Our first stop was the morgue.

"Good idea, Joe," Sunday told me. "Looking for a body in the morgue, I mean. Reminds me of how I looked for a needle in a haystack when I was a kid. Got straw down my back. Itched like anything. Ever have that happen to you, Joe? You just itch and itch until you think you're going to go—"

"Crazy?" I said.

"Right," he said.

We stepped into the morgue. The coroner was working in the corner. He looked up.

"Hello, boys," he greeted us. "You must be here about that Potter's Field case." He rolled out one of the big drawers. "Name was Iscariot. Hanged himself. What do you want with him?"

"We don't," I said. "We're after a rabbi. Approximately age thirty-three. Died last Friday."

He shook his head. "Nothing like that here, Joe. We had two thieves last Friday, but no rabbis. Sorry."

"Guess the morgue is a dead end, Joe," Sunday said after we left. "Where to now?"

"The tomb," I said.

"Why, Joe?"

I looked at him. He looked at me.

"To get the facts," I said.

Monday, April 7, 4:13 P.M. We pulled up at a rich man's tomb outside the city.

"These places give me the creeps, Joe," Sunday said. "Just like funerals. My wife went to a funeral the other day. They had those little unleavened crackers with olives and mustard seeds and things on them. She hates green olives. You know the kind, Joe? They're too—"

"Salty?" I said.

"Right," he said. "And—"

"Halt!" said a voice behind us. "This tomb is off limits, by order of the governor!"

We turned around. There were two Roman soldiers—one tall, one short. We flashed our badges.

"Cops!" gasped the tall one.

"Remember what we practiced," the short one whispered. Their eyes shifted back and forth. "Uh—we don't know what happened," the tall one whined. "We were guarding the tomb. It was all sealed and everything. Then we fell asleep."

"Right," the short one broke in. "There was definitely *not* a man in a shining robe who appeared and scared us so much that we fainted."

"Yeah," said the tall one. "The rabbi's disciples came while we were asleep and stole the body."

"Right," the short one agreed. "We know that because—because we were asleep at the time."

"And nobody bribed us to say that or anything," the tall one added.

"Makes sense to me, Joe," Sunday said.

"How do you two know this rabbi was dead in the first place?" I asked.

"Oh, he was dead, all right," the tall one answered. "I checked him myself, right after the execution."

"So he couldn't have come back to life," said the short one. "We know, because we were there."

"Sleeping," added the tall one.

"Well, Joe," Sunday said, "there it is. The rabbi's disciples stole the body. Guess that wraps it up, eh?"

"Not quite," I told him. "We're still missing one thing."

"What's that, Joe?"

"Proof," I said.

Thursday, April 10, 2:14 P.M. We ran down a lead in Emmaus. Two suspects had been seen proceeding down the road—right after the rabbi's body was stolen.

"You think they took the body, Joe?" Sunday asked.

"Could be," I said. "They're religious fanatics. Watch your step."

We walked up to the door. When I knocked, a teenager answered. He smiled as we flashed our badges.

"Come in," he invited. We did.

"Were you on the road to Emmaus the other day, son?" I questioned.

"That's right," he told me excitedly. "That's when we saw the—"

"Mind if we have a look around?" I asked.

"Go ahead," he said. "Anyway, we saw the—"

"There's no rabbi in here, Joe," Sunday said, peering into the closet.

"We *saw* the rabbi," the kid claimed. "The one who died last Friday. I was on the road with a friend, and we *saw* him. He's alive!"

I looked at Sunday. He looked at me. I shook my head.

"Consumption of new wine by a minor," I said. "That's against the law, son."

"But I didn't—"

"It's a 427, Joe," Sunday said. "I think."

"It's always the same story with you kids," I complained. "You go out and get yourself full of new wine and end up

114   Joan 'n' the Whale

seeing dead rabbis walking down the road. It's a shame, a real shame."

"But we *saw* him," the kid said. "We didn't recognize him at first. Then right before he disappeared—"

"Disappeared?" I asked.

"That's right. He vanished into thin air."

I looked at Sunday. He looked at me. We both shook our heads.

"You—you don't believe me," the kid exclaimed.

I frowned. "There's only one thing we believe, son," I said.

"The facts, Joe?" Sunday said.

"The facts," I said.

Tuesday, April 15, 9:48 P.M. We staked out the upper room. Word was that the rabbi's disciples had been hiding there—probably hiding the stolen body there, too. We parked in a nearby alley and watched as a sleazy collection of fishermen, women, zealots, and tax collectors went into the place, one by one.

"As long as we're waiting, Joe," Sunday said, "you mind if I have a bite?" He took a bag out of his pocket. "My wife made it, Joe. Barley cakes and figs. Don't care for figs. Too wrinkly. I like those other things, those—"

"Dates?" I queried.

"Right," he said.

"It's time," I told him. "Let's move in and wrap up this case."

"Can I finish my barley cakes, Joe? I'll—"

I looked at him. He looked at me.

"Right, Joe," he said. "After we get—"

"The facts," I said.

Tuesday, April 15, 9:59 P.M. It sounded as if a party was going on in the upper room. When I knocked, a young woman opened the door. "Yes?" she asked.

Joan 'n' the Whale

"Police officers," I announced, flashing my badge. "We have a few questions."

"Certainly," she responded, smiling. "What would you like to know?"

My eyes narrowed. "Just the facts, ma'am," I said.

"Well, come right in," she invited.

We walked in. I held up my badge.

"Party's over folks," I said. "You're all under arrest for theft and concealment of a body with intent to perpetuate a rumor about a resurrected rabbi. You have the right to remain silent. You have the right to—"

"Say, Joe," Sunday said. "How come nobody's listening?"

I stopped. Nobody *was* listening. They were too busy celebrating something.

There were all those disciples, talking and laughing with a guy in the middle of the room. A guy they kept calling "rabbi." A guy about thirty-three years old, wearing a white robe. A guy with a nasty scar in the palm of each hand, just as if he'd been—

I looked at Sunday. He looked at me.

"It's him, Joe," he said.

"That's right," I said.

"He doesn't look dead to me, Joe."

"No, he doesn't."

"What do we do now, Joe?"

I sighed. "You know procedure," I told him. "We make our report."

"But Joe—"

"I know," I said. "There's just one problem."

"What's that, Joe?" he asked.

"The facts," I said. "Just the facts."

Wednesday, April 16, 10:17 A.M. We finished making our report to the captain.

"So, boys," he said, looking it over. "The rabbi's followers stole the body, eh?"

"Yes, sir," I said. "Smuggled it out of the country. Way out. Out of our jurisdiction."

"They *did?*" Sunday asked. "But Joe, I thought—"

"It's just as well," the captain said. "The whole thing will blow over in a week or two anyway."

I nodded. "No doubt about it, sir," I answered.

"But how about all those sightings?" queried the captain. "What made so many people claim to have seen this man alive?"

"Yeah, Joe," Sunday said. "How—"

"Mass hypnosis, sir," I explained. "Swamp gas. Hysteria. It's all in the report."

"Oh," said Sunday. "I guess we were—"

"Mistaken?" I asked.

"Uh, right," he said.

"Good work, boys," congratulated the captain. "I knew I could count on you to get—"

"The facts, sir?" I asked.

"No," said the captain. "Something far better."

"What's that?" I wondered aloud.

"A *reasonable explanation.*"

"Makes sense to me, Joe," said Sunday.

"It would," I said with a sigh.

23 The Whole Armor

"**M**ay I *help* you?" came an oily voice from behind the counter.

The young man looked around the little clothing shop. "I'm looking for an outfit," he said. "I was headed for another shop, but it's too far away, and I was getting tired—"

"*Perfectly* understandable," lisped the voice. Its owner, a waxen-faced salesman with slicked-back dark hair and hollow cheeks, finally rose from behind the counter. "I'm sure we can help you with any wardrobe you could have found at that *other* store," he promised, rubbing his hands together. "And at a better price, no doubt."

"I sure hope so," said the young man. "I hear the price at that other store is pretty high. They want practically everything you've got."

"Tsk, tsk," went the salesman, gathering up his measuring tape. "Imagine the *nerve* of that other store, claiming to be the only *official* outfitter—and then charging the highest prices in town." He walked over to the young man, positioned him in front of a three-way mirror, and smiled. "What sort of outfit would you like?" he asked.

"A suit of armor," said the young man.

The salesman arched an eyebrow. "A suit of *what?*"

"Armor. See, I just joined up to fight the battle, and they gave me this list of armor I'm supposed to wear." He held up a piece of paper.

"Oh, *that* armor," said the salesman, reading. "Of course. We have an old suit like that in the back, I believe. But take my word for it—you wouldn't like it."

"Why not?"

The salesman sniffed. "It's simply *gauche*," he replied. "No one would be caught *dead* in a suit like that these days."

"But I'm supposed to *get* one," the young man protested. " 'Put on the whole armor,' they told me. They said I couldn't fight the battle without it."

The salesman sighed. "Oh, very well," he said. "What do you need first?"

The young man looked at his piece of paper. "The Girdle of Truth," he read.

"A *girdle?*" the salesman cried.

The young man blushed. "Well, it says right here that I have to gird my loins with truth. Have you got one or not?"

"Just a *minute*," the salesman said, rolling his eyes and disappearing into the back room. In a moment he appeared with a wide leather band.

"Ouch," cried the young man, putting it around his waist. "It feels awfully tight. Haven't you got it in a larger size?"

"Sorry," said the salesman. "You know how truth is. One size supposedly fits all. So *constricting*, don't you think?"

"Yeah, I guess so," the young man agreed woefully. "But they said I had to gird up my loins, so—"

"We *do* have an alternative," the salesman offered. "It's the Belt of Regulations." He pulled a heavy plastic band from a shelf. "A lovely piece of work, studded with artificial do's and don'ts."

The young man tried it on. "Ow!" he said. "This one's even worse. It's so tight I can barely breathe."

"Some *prefer* that hidebound feeling," the salesman explained. "But I have something else that may be more to your liking." He reached under the counter and produced a piece of string.

"What's that?" the young man asked.

"The Sash of Sincerity," answered the salesman. "Try it on. I think you'll find it quite comfortable."

"Feels fine," the young man said. Then he frowned. "But they told me I couldn't fight the battle if I didn't gird up my—"

"*Exactly*," the salesman said. "How can you fight a battle with a tight old belt around your waist? You need room to move, to slide, to waffle. The Sash of Sincerity is every bit as good as the Girdle of Truth and a lot more fashionable. Who needs truth if you're sincere?"

"Well . . . ," said the young man. "I—I guess that makes sense. I'll take the sash."

"An *excellent* choice," he gushed. "What's next?"

The young man checked his list. "The Breastplate of Righteousness," he read.

"Ugh," the salesman said.

"What's the matter?"

He shook his head. "You'll absolutely *hate* it," he promised. "An ugly old thing, probably rusty by now. Weighs a ton. They've been out of style for *ages.*"

"But my list says—"

He sighed. "I know, I know," he said, and went into the back room. Soon the sounds of grunting and clunking could be heard as he carried a large iron breastplate onto the sales floor. "See?" he said, huffing and puffing. He dropped the breastplate to the floor with a clang.

"It *does* look kind of uncomfortable," the young man agreed. "But how could I go into battle without it?"

The salesman snapped his fingers. "By wearing the Straitjacket of *Self*-righteousness," he declared. He took a box from a shelf and helped the young man put on its contents. "There," he said. "How's that?"

The young man tried in vain to move his arms. "It's lighter than that iron thing," he said. "But I don't think I could put up much of a fight without my hands. Feels kind of stiff, too—sort of like a stuffed shirt."

The salesman nodded. "I know *exactly* what you mean," he purred. He reached into a nearby rack and pulled out a red sports shirt. "Try this instead," he suggested.

"Hey, I like this," the young man said. "But how can this take the place of the Breastplate of Righteousness?"

The salesman chuckled. "Look at the insignia over the pocket."

The young man squinted at the mirror. "Is it an alligator?" he asked.

"*No,*" the salesman scoffed. "It's a *smiley face.* The international symbol of—"

"Righteousness?"

"No, *niceness.* You're wearing the Sports Shirt of Niceness. A perfect substitute. With that bright red color, the enemy will *never* notice you sneaking through the forest."

"Really?"

"Trust me," he said, rubbing his hands.

"The Shoes of the Gospel," continued the young man.

"Right here." The salesman pointed to a pair of black boots in a display case. "The most unattractive footwear known to man. Tell me, wouldn't you rather wear those nice running shoes you've got on?"

"Well, yeah, I guess I would. But they told me—"

"Of *course* they did," the man said. "They were probably jealous of your fine shoes. Let me show you what you really need—the *Shoestrings* of the Gospel." He handed the young man a pair of laces with tiny crosses printed all over them. "You can wear your own comfortable shoes and make a statement at the same time. Aren't they *marvelous?*"

The young man frowned. "I . . . don't know," he said. "I'd feel kind of silly wearing these things. I mean, somebody might *see* them."

"My thoughts *precisely,*" the salesman said. "That's why I've got something even better. The *Socks* of the Gospel."

"The *what?*"

"Take a look. One hundred percent cotton, with the same

design as the shoelaces. But who's to see? They'll be hidden away in those comfy shoes of yours."

The young man examined them. "How much do they cost?" he asked.

"A pittance," the salesman told him. "Only a fraction of what you'd pay for those ugly shoes."

"Well, okay," the young man said. "Now I need the Shield of Faith."

The salesman laughed. "My boy, you may need faith, but you *don't* need a shield. Nobody's used a shield for centuries. War isn't fought with bows and arrows anymore. This is the atomic age."

"Oh. Then what do I need?"

"The *Sunglasses* of Faith," explained the salesman. "For shielding your eyes on the battlefield. Here, try these."

The young man put on the glasses. "I can't see a thing," he cried. "These sunglasses are pitch black."

"Naturally," said the salesman. "They're for *blind* faith."

"I can't go into battle with these," the young man argued. "Guess I'll have to stick with the shield."

"You want a shield?" the man asked. "I'll give you a shield. But not one of those big bronze things. Have a button instead." He pulled a carton from a shelf.

"A button?"

"They're shaped just like shields, only much smaller. You can pin them right on your shirt. They're the Buttons of Belief."

"But I need *faith.*"

"Faith, belief—they're both the same. Just look at the wonderful slogans on these buttons: 'HONK IF YOU BELIEVE.' 'I BELIEVE IT, I BELIEVE IT, THAT SETTLES IT.' 'TURN YOUR SCARS INTO CANDY BARS.' "

The young man picked a bright yellow button. "I like this one," he said. "It says, 'MAKE BELIEVE, NOT WAR.' "

"It's *you,*" agreed the salesman.

"Next, the Helmet of Salvation," the young man read.

"Take my word for it," the salesman said. "That helmet is a dog. Like having a galvanized bucket on your head. Anyway, what's the important thing about salvation?"

"Spending eternity with—"

"No," the man cut him off. *"Security* is what everybody wants. That's exactly what you get with the Headband of Security." He picked it up from the counter. "Absorbent terry cloth. Keeps you dry in the heat of battle. That's the kind of protection you *really* need."

"A *headband?* I don't know. Seems like—"

"Then try the Hairspray of Holiness. *So* much lighter than that miserable helmet."

"Holiness, huh? They told me I'd need that, too."

"It's artificial, of course. But who'll know the difference?" The salesman picked up a can and sprayed it in the air. "Look at that," he said. "Makes a lovely halo effect when the light hits it just right, don't you think?"

"Yeah, but . . . I'll take the headband," the young man said.

"Very good," said the salesman. "That leaves—don't tell me—the Sword of the Spirit."

"Right."

"Much too expensive, I'm afraid. Useless, too. Fine for museums, but not much else. I have something better."

"What's that?"

He pointed to a gleaming object on a shelf. "The Brass Knuckles of Doctrine. They don't pierce quite like the old swords did, but they're wonderful for pummeling."

The young man looked doubtful. "I could really use something *sharper,"* he said. "After all, this is war."

The salesman stroked his chin with a bony finger. "Sharper," he repeated. "Of *course.* What you need is the Tie Tack of Tolerance." He took a tiny bauble from the jewelry case. "Our designers have managed to reduce the Sword of the Spirit to this size for ornamental purposes. But of course there's still a bit of a stickpin on the back."

The young man looked it over. "But I could never do battle with this. It would barely draw blood."

The salesman shuddered. "*Blood?* Young man, we are talking about *fashion* here." He motioned toward the mirror. "Just look at you. You'll be the envy of everyone on the battlefield. You've got the Sash of Sincerity, the Sports Shirt of Niceness, the Socks of the Gospel, the Button of Belief, the Headband of Security, and the Tie Tack of Tolerance. What more could any soldier want?"

The young man admired himself. "I *do* look pretty good, don't I?" he said. "I guess you're right. I'll take the whole armor—er, outfit."

"Excellent!" said the salesman. "Will that be cash or charge?"

"Check," said the young man, tossing his list into the nearest trash can. He pulled out his checkbook. "Who do I make it out to?" he asked.

"B.L. Zeebub," said the salesman, rubbing his hands together.

The young man signed the check and handed it over. "I'll just wear the outfit home, I guess," he said.

"Oh, *good,*" said the salesman. "That will make things *so* much easier."

"Well, thanks," said the young man, turning to go. "Glad I came here instead of that *other* store."

"So am I," said the salesman, quietly taking a tiny bow and a fiery dart from under the counter. "So am *I.*"

24 The Boxing Match

Excitement filled the meeting hall as folks found their seats. "Oh, I *love* these get-togethers," bubbled a woman to her friend who sat nearby. "They're always so—so *inspirational.*"

"Absolutely," agreed her friend. "I just don't know what I'd do without them. Or without *him*, of course." She nodded reverently toward the small cardboard box that sat beside her on the bench. "I bring him with me wherever I go, you know. He makes me feel so—so *safe.*"

"I know what you mean," said the first woman, bringing a little flowered metal tin from her purse. "Just knowing he's there, all snug in this box, makes me so happy to be a boxholder. When I think back to the old days, before I even knew you could *put* him in a box—why, I don't know how I managed to keep going!"

"My thoughts *exactly,*" said her friend, patting the carton at her side. "Until I started coming here, I had no *idea* what he might be like. That's why it's so good to attend these meetings. We can learn so much from each other, don't you think?"

"No doubt about it," the first woman said. "Why, it's so interesting to—" She stopped as the organ music began. "Oh, here we go!" she whispered. "I can just feel my heart beating a mile a minute. Tonight's a sharing time, and that always makes me a little nervous."

Joan 'n' the Whale

"Now, now," whispered her friend. "Don't forget, *he's* right there with you." She pointed at the carton on the bench. "Yours *is* a friendly one, isn't he? I mean, he helps you when you're worried and all that?"

"Well, of *course*," the lady said. "I wouldn't want one of those *other* ones. Why, I knew a man who had one who—"

"*Ssshhh!*" interrupted an elderly gentleman from the bench behind her. "You're disturbing him." He patted the wooden box that sat on his lap. "He's very sensitive. Besides, the meeting is starting."

Sure enough, the organ music reached a crescendo at that very moment. The audience held its breath. Suddenly a dapper young man entered from the wings, flashed a brilliant smile, and took his place at the center of the platform.

"Good evening!" he said. "*So* nice to see you all here tonight—and so nice to see so many *wonderful* boxes!" He paused, his face growing somber. "You know, friends, we are *so* blessed. Some folks don't even know about—about *him*. They don't know you can tuck him away all safe and snug in your own personal container. Let's take a moment to thank him, shall we?"

All over the auditorium people turned to their boxes— small boxes, big boxes, metal, wood, and cardboard boxes—and gave them an affectionate pat. The young man in front took a sleek leather case from his suit pocket and gave it a heartfelt wink.

"*Such* a blessing," he said huskily and stuffed the case back into his pocket. Then he smiled again.

"Hey!" he enthused. "Let's get this show on the road. As you all know, one of the greatest things about getting together is sharing with each other what's in our boxes. Or rather *who's* in them. So tonight I'm going to pick a few of you at random to come right up here and tell us about the boxes you've brought."

Nervous whispers ran up and down the aisles as the young man scanned the audience. "Let's see," he said.

The Boxing Match

"How about this lady here in the third row—the one with the blue dress? Come on up!"

Giggling, a plump woman squeezed past the others in her row and made her way to the front. She was carrying a schoolgirl's lunch box that had pretty pink flowers on the side.

"Oh, I'm so excited!" she said when she reached the platform. "I've always wanted to get up here and tell everyone about—well, about You-know-who."

"Here's your chance," the young man offered, beaming. "Tell us about the box you've brought."

She held it up for all to see. "I keep him in a lunch box," she explained, "to remind me of how he gives me everything my heart desires. Like food, for instance."

"Very good!" the young man commended her. "Does he give you anything *besides* food?"

"Oh, my, yes," she rejoiced. "He showers down cars and boats and houses and nice clothes and good health and home computers and tax shelters and candy bars—"

"I see," the young man said with a chuckle. "Sounds like you've *really* got him in a box, all right!"

"I sure do!" She giggled. "It's so comforting to know he's there. He's done such a good job that one of these days I may even trade in his lunch box for a nice, roomy picnic basket!"

"Now *that's* a thoughtful idea," the young man approved. "I'm sure he'll appreciate that. Thanks so much for sharing. You can go back to your seat now, and I'll look for our next boxholder."

The woman returned to her seat as the young man scanned the audience again. "How about *this* man?" he asked pointing. "Toward the back, last seat on the right."

"*Me?*" came a nervous voice from the audience.

"Yes, you. Come right up here and tell us about your box."

"W-well, all right," said the man, reluctantly getting up and shuffling down the aisle. In his arms he cradled a large cardboard carton, which he kept glancing at anxiously.

"That's it," the young man soothed. "Just come right up here. No need to be frightened."

"That's what *you* think," the man quavered, watching his box as if it might explode any second. When he finally made it to the front, he was shaking.

"Now," said the young man, "that wasn't so bad, was it?"

"N-not yet," the man stammered. "B-but it could happen any time, you know."

The young man raised his eyebrows. *"What* could happen any time?"

"H-he could get mad," the man worried, peering at his box. "I n-never know when he might jump out and punish me. It hasn't happened yet, but when I least expect it, he could decide to hit me with lightning b-bolts or a disease or something."

The young man frowned at the box. "Why would he want to do *that?"*

"B-because he's like a policeman," the man blurted, sweat popping out on his forehead. "He's always watching me, waiting for me to do something wrong." He stared in horror at his box, talking faster and faster. "I can just feel him getting angry with me, and I always do something wrong because I'm such a bad person, and he's out to get me, and—and—*Aaauugghh!"* The screaming man leaped from the platform, ran down the aisle, and was gone.

"Well," continued the young man brightly after a pause. "As I always say, 'To thine own box be true'!" Smiling, he turned to the audience again. "Let's try another boxholder. How about you, ma'am, on the aisle? You look like you have something—or some*one*—to show us."

"I certainly do," said an attractive woman who came forward with a mirrored compact. "I just want to say that

I've kept You-know-who in this box for years, and he would *never* do anything to harm or upset me. We're the best of friends. It's *such* an encouragement to know that he wouldn't *dare* to irritate or contradict me."

"I know that's been true in my own life," the young man agreed earnestly, and many in the audience nodded. "What would you say is the secret of getting along so well with him?"

The woman thought for a moment. "I think," she finally responded, "it's the fact that he's growing to be more and more like me every day. Whenever I want to remind myself of what he's like, I just glance in the mirror on this compact—and there he is!"

The young man sighed knowingly and nodded. "What a sweet and precious truth!" he said. "Thank you *so* much for sharing." He took out a handkerchief and dabbed at his eyes as the woman returned to her seat. "Well, friends," he said with a sniffle and a smile, "let's have another boxholder come up and tell us what's in—"

"Stop!" yelled a voice from the back of the room. "I won't hear another word of this. Not another word!" The speaker, a stern, middle-aged man, came marching up the aisle, dragging a huge file cabinet behind him. "I've listened to this heresy long enough," he objected. "All this nonsense about 'You-know-who' and putting him in boxes. Who do you people think you *are?*"

"What do you mean?" the young man asked, flustered.

"You obviously have no conception of what he's *really* like," the man spoke out testily. "Lunch boxes, cartons, and compacts indeed. He's *much* too big for any of those things."

"He *is?*"

"That's right," the man said, proudly patting his file cabinet. "It's all right in here, in my doctrinal statement." He pulled a manila folder from the first drawer, cleared his throat, and began to read. "*I believe* in the pretribulational, predestinational foreknowledge of the dispensational, non-charismatic system of hermeneutics," he declared. *"I believe* in the substitutionary immersion of sanctification, edification, justification, the omnipresent, omniscient, omnipotent, triune. . . ."

The young man and the audience listened politely for the next half hour as the man read the entire contents of his file cabinet. Slowly, almost imperceptibly, a glorious light began to dawn in their eyes.

"Of course!" the young man cried when the reader was finished. "Why didn't we see this *before?* We've been so *blind!"*

"So blind!" agreed several in the audience.

The man with the file cabinet looked around with a superior air. "Well," he said smugly. "At least you *admit* your error."

"Indeed we do," the young man confessed ruefully. "But now we can change, thanks to you." He dabbed his eyes again. His face fairly glowed as he turned to the assembled boxholders. "My friends!" he exclaimed. "Through this man's shining example, we have seen how at last we may be free of our boxes! No longer need we carry these cumbersome containers around! As our visitor has shown, we can leave You-know-who at home—in a *file cabinet!"*

"W-What?" the man blustered. "But I—"

"Thank you *so* much for sharing that life-changing insight!" the young man said as the audience burst into spontaneous applause. "My friends!" the young man cried, glancing at his watch. "Once again our time has flown. Thank you all for being part of this *very* special evening—and don't forget your boxes!"

There was another round of applause as the organ music came up. The man with the file cabinet slowly walked down the aisle, bewildered.

"I just *love* these meetings," whispered the woman with

the cardboard box at her side. "So *inspirational*, you know."

"Isn't *that* the truth," said her friend. She glanced at the little flowered tin on her lap. "I think he'll look *lovely* in a file cabinet, don't you?" she asked.

"Divine," came the reply. "Absolutely *divine*."

25

The Witness

Oh, hi, officer.

Yeah, I saw the whole thing. This candy-apple-red Corvette came screaming around the corner and went through the stop sign. That old Nova was tooling up the street, minding its own business, and the Corvette plowed right into the side of it—*wham!*

It really was a mess. It's a wonder nobody got killed. That Corvette must have been going sixty miles an hour, weaving all over the road—

Huh? You want me to be a *what?* Oh, no way! I can't *witness.* Witnessing is for *other* people.

What other people? Well, people who are cut out for that sort of thing. You know—people who could jump right up there on the witness stand and tell what happened. You've got to have a way with words to witness, after all.

You say I'm the only one who *saw* the accident? Yeah, but . . . there must be plenty of other people who have seen *other* accidents. Maybe they didn't see *this* one, but that's not important, is it? I'll bet they could get right up there and tell the jury about *their* accidents. Wouldn't that be just as good?

No? Well, look . . . this accident wasn't all that spectacular. Get one of those other guys to testify—one who's seen a really dramatic head-on collision or a high-speed police chase or a big freeway pileup with lots of casualties. No jury would be interested in *my* story. They'd be bored to death.

No, I couldn't witness. I freeze up when I talk to groups. Sometimes I freeze up when I talk to just one *person*. What you need is my cousin Arnie. Now *that* guy could talk to anybody about anything. He's taken classes in public speaking, salesmanship, how to win friends and—

What? Well, of *course* Arnie didn't see the accident. But he's a great speaker!

Aw, come on. People would make fun of me. I'd get up there to tell my story, and some lawyer would make mincemeat out of my testimony. He'd say I didn't know what I was talking about. He'd say I was a hypocrite because I'd gotten a few traffic tickets myself. I'd be embarrassed in front of *everybody*.

What? That wouldn't *matter*? The important thing is just to tell my story?

Well . . . let's say for a minute that I *did* manage to say a *few* words in front of a *few* people. I'd be a flop. I don't know anything about skid marks and velocity and all that. I couldn't even quote more than a couple of lines from the driver's manual. I didn't study that stuff in school. I'd be *awful* at witnessing.

Another thing . . . what good would it do if I *did* testify? Nobody cares what I think. The two drivers always have their minds made up about who's to blame. I've never even *met* the judge or jury. I'd have to spend *years* getting to know them before I could ever talk to them about something as *personal* as this accident.

Huh? I'm an *expert* on what happened? Just because I was the only one who *saw* it?

Well . . . I'll tell you what. I'll do something *better* than witnessing. I'll print up a little pamphlet that talks about accidents and has lots of quotes from the driver's manual. Then you can stand on a street corner and pass it out to people as they go by.

No? Well, how about if I *pay* somebody to go on the witness stand and testify *for* me? Maybe a whole bunch of us who don't want to witness could pool our money and hire a guy like that. . . .

Aw, come on, officer. Give me a break. Why do you keep hassling me to witness?

What? You say I already *am* a witness?

But how can that be? I mean, isn't a witness somebody who *tells* about something?

He's what? A person who *witnesses* something? Sees it? Is there when it happens?

But . . . that means when I witnessed the accident, I became a. . . .

A witness.

Oh, man.

Say, officer. . . .

I don't suppose we could forget about the whole thing, could we?

Oh.

Somehow I knew you'd say that.

The Witness

26

The Conversion
of Paul Bunyan

He was such a . . . *little* guy.

That was the first thing I noticed when he came up to me on the street. Actually, he sort of popped out of an alley as I walked by. He looked like most of the winos in that neighborhood, gray haired, unshaven, and dressed in a tattered overcoat. He wasn't carrying a bottle, though. His eyes weren't all that bloodshot either; they just stared into the distance, kind of sad and empty.

He pulled off his grimy stocking cap and twisted it in his hands. That's when I figured he was going to ask me for money. But he didn't. He just stood there, as if waiting for me to say something.

"I haven't got any cash," I finally managed.

"Oh, that's all right," he said, looking up at me. I mean, he *really* looked up. I'm about six feet tall, and this guy couldn't have been more than four and a half feet. He was a little bent over, of course, which may have had something to do with it.

"So what do you want?" I asked, eager to move along.

He grabbed my sleeve. "Have—have you seen Babe?" he asked.

I raised an eyebrow. "Who?"

He motioned me into the alley. I followed him for a step or two. "I was not always as you see me now," he whispered urgently. "You must believe me."

Joan 'n' the Whale

"Okay," I humored him. "You used to be rich, right?"

"No, no," he said. "I used to be *taller*."

"Oh."

"Perhaps you've heard of me," he said. "My name is . . . Paul Bunyan."

I shook my head. "The only Paul Bunyan I ever heard of was in the tall tales we read in grade school."

"Yes, yes!" agreed the little man. "A giant logger from the North Woods. He leveled whole forests with one stroke of his ax. He had a big, blue ox named Babe."

"Right," I answered, looking at my watch.

"That's me," he said. "I'm Paul Bunyan."

I glanced down at him. "Excuse me," I protested, "but the Paul Bunyan I'm talking about was . . . well . . . a lot taller."

"I know," he wistfully acknowledged, staring past me. "I was so big that when I walked, lakes formed in my footprints. I ate flapjacks so huge that they had to be cooked on a griddle greased by men who skated on slabs of bacon. I had a laugh so hearty it could be heard from one end of the woods to the other—"

"Yeah, that's the one," I said. "But Paul Bunyan's just a tall tale—a folk hero. He's not *real.*"

He shook his head. "Do I look like a folk hero?" he asked.

"No," I admitted. "But Paul Bunyan was tall enough to touch the tops of the trees. You're so . . . *short.*"

He lowered his head. "I know," he mumbled. "That's because I got . . . converted."

"*Converted?*" I cried. "You mean . . . ?"

"Yes," he said, looking into the distance. "One Sunday morning about a year ago, Babe and I left the North Woods. We walked until we found a church; I knocked on the roof, and they sent out some men to talk to me. They wouldn't let me walk the aisle—said it wasn't wide enough. But that was the day I got converted."

The Conversion of Paul Bunyan   137

"Uh-huh," I responded doubtfully.

"They baptized me in the nearest lake," he went on. "I was so tall I flooded the banks. Fish were stacked ten feet deep around the shore when I got out."

"Right," I said, looking skeptical.

"The church building wasn't big enough for me, of course," he continued. "So Babe and I would sit on a hill next to the church, listening to the sermon over a loudspeaker. I didn't know the hymns, but I'd do my best to sing along."

For a second the little man almost looked happy, remembering. Then that look of despair came back into his eyes. "That's when—when it started," he said. "First the church people told me I was singing praises too loudly. It made the pews vibrate, they claimed. So I had to stop singing and just mumble the words."

"I see."

"Then they told me I couldn't dress like a lumberjack if I

Joan 'n' the Whale

was truly converted. They made me get rid of my plaid shirt, my suspenders, my overalls, my boots. . . . I had to wear a black suit instead." He paused, swallowing. "That's when I—I noticed it."

"Noticed what?"

"That I wasn't quite as tall as I used to be. It wasn't much of a difference—just a few feet. So I forgot about it—until. . . ."

"Until what?"

He looked down at his ill-fitting shoes. "Until they made me stay out of the woods."

I frowned. "Now why would they do that?"

"They said converted people shouldn't hang around with the rough types you find in the woods. Too many lumberjacks there."

"But *you* were a lumberjack," I said.

"Not anymore. They told me I couldn't talk or laugh or smell like a lumberjack now that I was converted. I had to stop yelling 'Timber' and start saying 'Amen.' I had to shave my beard and stop roaming the woods with Babe. They made me take a job as an insurance salesman and moved me to the suburbs."

"But how could you live there? Weren't you too big?"

He shook his head. "Every time I did something to fit in with the church people, I got smaller," he said sadly. "Finally I was down to their level. They seemed pleased, but I didn't feel like myself anymore."

I looked down my nose at the little man. "Do you expect me to believe that getting *converted* made you shorter?" I asked.

"Oh, no," he said. "It wasn't the conversion. It was having to be like the others. I had to *shrink* to *fit*."

I shook my head. "Look, Mr. Bunyan—or whatever your real name is—people don't end up on Skid Row just because they're *short*. What are you doing here?"

The little man's lip began to tremble. "They—they sent

Babe away," he explained softly. "They told me blue oxen just didn't fit into their theology. I've been wandering the country ever since, looking for my old companion—" His voice broke as a single tear trickled down his grizzled cheek.

I looked away. Sure, I felt sorry for the guy, but he was *crazy*. Everybody knew there was no Paul Bunyan. Everybody knew something like that could *never* happen.

I looked at my watch again. One way or another, I had to get out of there. "Uh, that sure is a sad story, Mr. . . . Bunyan," I said finally, backing out of the alley. "I'm afraid I haven't seen any giant blue oxen around here lately, though. You just keep looking, and I'm sure you'll find him—or her."

I tried to look hopeful. But when I left, the little man was sort of sagging against the wall, gazing up into the sky.

Whew, I thought, walking quickly down the street. *What a nut! Imagine, all that nonsense about shrinking to fit in. . . .*

Good thing I'd been able to get away. After all, I couldn't be seen talking to somebody like *that*. I mean, what would people from *church* think?

27

Return of the
Living Dead

"*Lazarus, come forth!*"

Huh? Wha—

Hey. I thought I was . . . sleeping. How come my mattress is so hard all of a sudden? Feels like a—

Well, what do you know? It *is* a rock. What am I doing lying on a rock?

How come it's so dark in here? What's this cloth on my face? It's almost as if I were—

Oh, that's right.

I *was* . . . dead.

Dead? Well, then how can I be—

"*Lazarus, come forth!*"

What's all the noise? It's loud enough to raise the—

Oh. Somebody's yelling at *me*. Now why would anybody yell at a *dead* person? Can't I get any peace and quiet *anywhere?*

"*Lazarus, come forth!*"

Wait a minute. I recognize that voice. What's *he* doing here? Where was he when I *needed* him? Probably off somewhere healing the lepers, making the lame walk and the blind see. All the while I was dying. *Now* he shows up. What perfect timing.

"Lazarus, come forth!"

He wants me to come *out?* What is he, crazy? Dead people don't come out of their tombs. Especially not after three days. Where does he think they got that saying, "Rest in peace"? Doesn't he have any respect for the dead?

Hey, wait. Did I imagine that, or did I just move my finger? There, I did it again. There's something strange going on here. Dead people don't move their fingers—or anything else.

"Lazarus, come forth!"

What's going on here? I just wiggled my foot. There's a pattern developing. I must be . . . *alive!*

Oh, great. Here I was, nice and dead, minding my own business—and all of a sudden I have to come back to life. Whose idea *was* this?

"Lazarus, come forth!"

I should have known. This is just the sort of thing he'd do. He's always telling people "Follow me," or, "Sell all you have and give to the poor," or, "Go and sin no more." Always calling and changing and sending, never leaving well enough alone. Did he *ask* me whether I wanted to come back from the dead? *Nooooo.* Did he think for a moment of *my* comfort and well-being? Of *course* not.

"Lazarus, come forth!"

I suppose he thinks it's so great out there that I should *jump* at the chance to come out. But he just doesn't realize how *nice* it is in here. It's so quiet—or at least it was before he started shouting. And I like the decor—simple, with lots of earth tones. No bad weather, no sunburn, no worries about what Martha might cook for dinner. . . .

"Lazarus, come forth!"

No having to decide every day what I'll wear. These wrappings *are* a little tight, but then who needs mobility if you're not going anywhere? There's a certain comfort in always knowing where you'll be. And it's so *safe* here. Or at least it would be if they'd roll that stone back where it's *supposed* to be.

"Lazarus, come forth!"

What's this "come forth" business? What does he *want* from me, anyway? The minute I stepped out of here, he'd probably want me to *do* something for him, I'll bet. Well, he can forget that. *This* is where I belong, right here with my comfortable slab and graveclothes, like any *normal* person.

"Lazarus. . . ."

Well, it's about time. He's finally given up! Sure took him long enough.

What's that noise? Ah, they're finally rolling the stone back into place. Now maybe I can get some *rest*.

Wow, it really *is* dark in here.
And quiet—*real* quiet.
And cool, and—and—

Say . . . what's that awful *smell?*

Return of the Living Dead   143

28

The Church in Harmony🖋

 It was a church in Harmony, all right.

In fact, it was the *only* church in Harmony, a little town I'd pulled into just moments before. I was admiring the church's shining steeple and freshly painted white clapboard siding when a young man came out to greet me.

"Welcome!" he said, and smiled. "Will you be joining us this morning?"

"Well, sure," I answered. "I'm just passing through on business, but since it's Sunday morning—"

"Wonderful!" he enthused. "We're glad to have you. You're a bit early, though; service won't start for a few minutes. Since it's such a nice day, why don't we just stand out here and chat?"

"Sounds fine," I said, glancing around. "I was just admiring your building. Looks perfect as a postcard."

"Thank you. We like it, too. As you can see from the cornerstone, Harmony Community Church was built in 1879. It's not too big, but it seems just right for us. We try to be big enough to serve people, but small enough to know them."

"That's good," I said. Just then I happened to glance past the big oak doors into the foyer. There I noticed a picture on the wall, hung in a fancy, gilt-edged frame. It was a portrait of a rather large, stern-faced woman.

Joan 'n' the Whale

"Who's that?" I asked.

"Oh," the young man answered quietly, respectfully. "You mean Miss Bertha June Biggs. She was a very special person, you know."

"No, I didn't know."

"Oh, yes, Miss Bertha June Biggs was our founder, in a manner of speaking. We owe a lot to her. Almost single-handedly, she made Harmony Community Church the peaceful, beautiful place it is today."

"You don't say. How did she do that?"

The young man smiled and got a faraway look in his eyes. "Miss Biggs was a lady with the courage of her convictions," he said. "She never hesitated to stand up for what she knew was right. She opposed the forces of evil wherever they were found—even when they were found in the church."

My eyebrows went up. "Evil?" I asked. "In *this* church?"

"Oh, yes, indeed. Miss Bertha June Biggs had uncanny spiritual sensitivity. She could always tell if something was wrong in the church—even if everyone else thought things were fine. It takes a very spiritual person to do that, don't you think?"

"It certainly does," I said.

He leaned against the wall. "Take those preachers, for instance," he said earnestly. "Miss Biggs was here when Harmony got its very first pastor. He was fresh out of Bible school, and the whole congregation was grateful to get him. All except Miss Biggs, of course. She knew what was *really* going on."

"She did?"

"Naturally. She knew that young pastor was wet behind the ears. He couldn't *possibly* know how to run a church." His voice dropped to a whisper. "He also wanted to do all kinds of terrible things."

I leaned closer. "Like what?"

"Like electrifying the pump organ!" he cried. "Can you

believe it? Miss Biggs knew that would never do. It would lead to a weakening of the organist's ankles and probably the congregation's morals as well. You can see that, I'm sure."

"Well, I—"

"Anybody could," he said. "Fortunately the board of deacons saw it, too, when Miss Biggs pointed it out to them. They got rid of that pastor, so the church and the organist would remain strong."

"Oh," I said.

He sighed. "Unfortunately, the organist was too unspiritual to see the value of strong ankles, and she quit. But Miss Biggs knew that was fine, because the organist had always endangered the congregation's hearing by playing too loud, soft, high, low, fast, or slow—and by making a racket when she turned the pages of her sheet music. But that wasn't the worst of it."

"Oh?"

"She hardly *ever* played Miss Biggs's favorite hymns," he said. "Nor did the organist realize the danger of singing the 'Amens' at the ends of songs, which Miss Biggs knew was unhealthy—except of course in the case of the Doxology."

"Uh . . . of course."

"After that, another pastor came to Harmony. He was the Reverend Peachtree, Miss Biggs's favorite. She approved of him for the first twenty-three hours or so—but then he stood up to preach. Miss Biggs could see right away that he wasn't going to work out."

"Why?"

"Because he moved his arms too much when he talked. Just *watching* him made people tired, Miss Biggs said, and would cause them to fall asleep during sermons. And he didn't use enough illustrations about street urchins. Miss Biggs loved street urchins, you know. Not the actual urchins—she'd read you could get a disease or something if you got too close to them. But she loved to hear about them in sermon illustrations."

"I see."

"Still, she could have ignored all the Reverend Peachtree's shortcomings—if not for the shocking thing he did at the end of his very first sermon."

"What was that?"

The young man gazed at the picture on the wall, shaking his head in sympathy for what Miss Biggs had been forced to endure. "The Reverend Peachtree went *six minutes overtime*," he intoned, incredulous. "With her spiritual insight and all, Miss Biggs knew he had to go."

I stared at the picture, too. "What did she do to get rid of him?" I asked.

The young man gasped. "Get *rid* of him?" he cried. "Miss Bertha June Biggs never 'got rid of' anybody. She simply exercised her discernment, as was her duty." He paused and regained his composure. "She wrote some thoughtful, anonymous letters to Reverend Peachtree, suggesting that he explore some of the marvelous opportunities available in other parts of the country. He must have appreciated her helpfulness, because he left within the month."

"Naturally," I said.

"Then came the next pastor, a Reverend Trimble. He met Miss Biggs's common-sense standards for preaching. But he had an unfortunate quirk that could have ruined the church if left unchecked."

"What was that?"

The young man frowned. "An obsession with missions."

"You mean Miss Biggs didn't like missions?"

My informant threw up his hands. "Of *course* she liked missions. Why, her favorite song was 'From Greenland's Icy Mountains,' which she successfully requested every Sunday night. But the Reverend Trimble didn't understand missions at all; he was always trying to convince people to *be* missionaries, which Miss Biggs knew perfectly well was heresy."

"Oh," I said.

"Nor did she like it when the Reverend Trimble invited all those missionaries to come and show their slides of foreigners and other things that were best left to *National Geographic*. One Sunday night a visiting missionary showed so many slides there was no time left to sing 'From Greenland's Icy Mountains.' Miss Biggs knew the kind of harm that sort of thing could do to a church, so she made sure Reverend Trimble left, too."

"Hmm," I said. "She must have had a high position on the church board."

"Sadly, no," the young man said. "It was hard just to get the board's attention, since they were always busy wasting the church's money, taking offerings for unnecessary things like roof patching and gas bills. One year they even wanted to get new pews!"

"Really," I said.

"Miss Biggs knew the old ones were perfectly fine. As she told the board, if the congregation would just wear thicker clothing, the splinters would be no problem at all."

"And did they?"

"The truly spiritual ones did. But quite a few backsliders—no pun intended—chose the coward's way out and left the church. That upset the board, so they resigned, too."

"That's terrible!"

"Oh, no, not at all. Miss Bertha June Biggs's campaign of purification was succeeding. By now no preacher dared venture near Harmony, having heard of Miss Biggs's exacting spiritual standards."

"Was that good?"

"Of course! That meant she could turn her attention from removing preachers and deacons to removing members of the congregation who failed to measure up. Now *there* was a task. Most members had already left—no doubt recognizing their spiritual inferiority—but there were still a few left to weed out."

"Such as?"

He thought for a moment. "I remember reading in the records of a Claude P. Flackberry, Sr. His prayers were always too long. He'd go on and on about the sick and the lame, the needy and the hungry, the lost and the destitute—all things Miss Biggs knew should not interest a good churchgoer. Fortunately, he passed on before he could lead the rest of the members astray."

"And the others?"

"They were everyday 'wolves in sheep's clothing,' as Miss Biggs called them. She graciously helped speed them on their way by letting the townspeople know what sins these members had confessed at prayer meeting. She had a verse for it, of course: '. . . That which ye have spoken in the ear in closets shall be proclaimed upon the house tops.' I believe that's Luke 12:3—King James Version, of course. Miss Biggs was always very careful with her use of Scripture."

"So I see."

"After these impure elements were removed, the Harmony Community Church was able to rest in peace at last. Miss Bertha June Biggs had finally transformed it into a truly harmonious body."

"How many members of this body were left?"

He beamed. "Just one—Miss Bertha June Biggs."

"And where is she?"

"When her job in Harmony was done, she moved away. She went to another church, I expect."

I scratched my head. "I don't understand," I said. "Miss Biggs *killed* the church. I thought you said she made it what it is today."

"I did," the young man replied. "It's a place that's 'big enough to serve you, small enough to know you.' Why, it's the finest restaurant in all of Harmony."

I blinked. "Restaurant?"

"Well, of course," he said. "Once the building was empty, my partners and I couldn't let it go to waste, could we? It's solid as a rock and pretty as a picture." He knocked his knuckles on the clean, white siding.

"But I . . . didn't see a sign," I objected slowly.

He nodded. "There's just a small, tasteful one on the other side of the building. Don't want to look *too* commercial, you know."

"Of course not," I replied faintly.

"So," he said cheerfully, "shall I seat you now? I'm sure our food service has gotten underway. We have a lovely Sunday brunch. The salad bar is where the pulpit used to be. You'll find the sunlight streaming through the stained glass is just—"

"Uh, no . . . no, thank you," I said, feeling numb. "I—I have to be going."

"Oh," he said, disappointed. "Well, do keep us in mind."

"I will," I promised, walking to my car. "Believe me, I will."

"Good!" he called after me. "And if you ever hear of any other churches that are being . . . *purified*, be sure to let us know."

I turned around. "Why?" I asked.

"Because," he said, smiling. "We're thinking of opening a *chain!*"

I shuddered.

It'll never work, I thought. But as I drove away, passing that peaceful little church in Harmony, I just couldn't be sure.

29 The Man Who Loved Porcupines🌿

You know that doctor down on Seventh Street? The so-called heart specialist? Yeah, that's the one. If you ever have a problem, don't go to see *him*. The guy's a quack. I mean, I went to him with this problem, but he couldn't fix it. Cost me twenty-five bucks to see him, and all he did was throw up his hands as if there were nothing he could do!

It went like this. I sat down on the examination table, and he asked, "So, what seems to be the problem?"

I explained, "Well, doc, I don't know exactly. I keep having these pains in my chest. Shooting pains. Maybe it's my heart."

"Hmm," he muttered. "Take off your shirt, and I'll have a listen."

So I took off my shirt. As soon as I did, this guy just about had a heart attack himself. "Hey!" he said. "What are all those puncture wounds on your chest?"

"Oh, they're nothin'," I breezed.

"Nothing?" he protested. "Son, those are serious wounds. There must be two dozen of them."

"Not counting the ones in my arms," I added.

He looked at my arms and whistled. Then he frowned. "All right," he said. "What happened?"

"Nothin', really. Just a porcupine, that's all."

"A porcupine?" he cried. "Son, to get this many wounds,

you'd have to pick up a porcupine with your bare hands and *hug* it."

"Right," I said. "That's what I did."

He looked at me with a really weird expression. "You *hugged a porcupine?*" he questioned. "Why would you want to do a thing like that?"

I shrugged. "I'm just into that, I guess. I like porcupines."

He took off his glasses and looked down his nose at me—just like my old man always does. "Son," he said, "you just can't *do* that. Porcupines aren't good for you. They're dangerous. They can stick you full of quills."

"So?" I said. "Don't knock it until you've tried it."

He shook his head. "I don't *have* to try it to know it's not good for me. Now promise me you'll stay away from porcupines."

"Hey," I said. "Are you a heart specialist or not? I've got chest pains. What are you going to do about it?"

That's when he threw up his hands. "There's nothing I *can* do, unless you give up hugging porcupines," he said. Then he put a bandage on my chest and sent me out the door.

Can you *believe* that guy? I mean, talk about self-righteous! Where does *he* get off judging my life-style? If I want to hug porcupines, that's *my* business. *His* job is to get rid of chest pains!

Anyway, I left and went over to the zoo. Sure enough, there were some great porcupines there. I sneaked into the cage, picked one up, and for some reason those chest pains started again. I mean, I thought I was gonna *die.*

So that's why I'm here, doc. You're a heart specialist, too, right? You've gotta help me. Maybe I need open heart surgery or a transplant or something, huh?

What? You want me to see the guy next door? What kind of doctor is *he?*

Well, why *won't* you tell me? What's—

Hey, who are these guys coming through the door?

Where are you taking me? I don't *want* to put on that jacket—

You people are all alike! Trying to crush my alternative life-style, imposing your worn-out morality! I'll get you for this! I'll—I'll—

Wait!

I'll . . . uh . . . make you a deal.

No more heart specialists.

How about lots of . . . acupuncture?

30

Angels We
Have Heard on High

Young Pastor Torgenson, resplendent in the new three-piece, charcoal-gray suit his wife had given him especially for this Christmas Eve service, mounted the platform. An ocean of faces looked back at him—the faces of the Red Ridge Community Church, holiday-excited and ruddy from the cold outside.

The pastor smiled for a second at his wife, who beamed from the first row; then he began. "Before the choir sings our anthem, 'Angels We Have Heard on High,'" he said, "let me remind you of a Scripture passage about angels. Turn with me to Hebrews 13:2, if you will. . . ."

A tissue-thin shuffle of Bible pages went through the sanctuary like a rushing wind. Then it stopped, and as the pastor was about to read Hebrews 13:2 a murmur rose in the rear pews near the door.

To the consternation of several older members, a shocking pair of visitors had entered. The man was tall, blond, bushy bearded—a near skeleton in a grimy navy pea coat. The girl was very, very pregnant, swathed in a shapeless beige peasant dress and tattered sweater. A kerchief failed to conceal her stringy black hair.

"Wonder if they're married?" whispered a woman in the back row.

"I never saw the like, not in this church," grumbled a

Joan 'n' the Whale

man. From her usual seat, old Mizzie Everett just squinted at the strangers, apparently as confused as ever.

Pastor Torgenson paused, smelling trouble. *Another battle of the old and the new,* he sighed to himself. Would it never end?

"Welcome," he finally called out to the bedraggled strangers. "We're glad you're here. Sit right down."

But it was easier said than done. The young couple had to wind their way to the front to find the only vacant seats. A few hundred curious eyes watched.

"Now, as I was saying," the young preacher continued, "Hebrews 13:2." He cleared his throat. "Do not forget to entertain strangers, for by so doing some people have entertained angels without knowing it."

He gulped, surprised at the verse's sudden aptness. "Well. Uh, perhaps you've read stories about Christmas visitations by angels. Many have been written, most of them pure fiction. But let's remember tonight that our Lord himself was not recognized for whom he was. And let's make sure there's room at *our* inn tonight." A nod to the choir and he sat down by the pulpit.

The music billowed behind him. He tried not to stare at the young couple, but couldn't help it. Who were they? Why were they here?

All at once it hit him. On Christmas Eve, a bearded young man and a pregnant young woman seeking shelter? Did they have a donkey parked outside, too?

He smiled to himself. "Entertained angels without knowing it"? Well, one never knew. . . .

The choir's last "Gloria in excelsis deo" faded, and the pastor jumped to his feet. He had an idea.

"In our bulletin, the order of service calls next for a pastoral prayer. But before I lead us, let's find out what we have to pray about on this Christmas Eve. Jack—" He motioned to an usher. "If you'll get the movable microphone, we can have a brief time of sharing our needs."

Again the pastor tried not to gaze at the young strangers, but hoped they'd share their obvious needs. After all, this was a unique chance for the church to show hospitality, he thought.

"Just a *brief* time," he repeated, unconsciously nodding at old Mizzie Everett in the back. Poor old Mizzie, they called her. She loved sharing times. At the first click of the microphone, she'd jump up as quickly as her arthritis allowed, only to ramble on and on about some long-forgotten event or person. The whole congregation would look at the floor, embarrassed, as Mizzie tried to remember a Bible verse or sing a song in her rusty squeal of a voice. It was starting to put a damper on services, some people said.

The pastor's hopes rose as the bearded young man started to get to his feet. But Mizzie was up first, and she took the microphone from the reluctant usher. An almost audible groan went up from the congregation.

"Uh, thank you, Mizzie," the pastor said after a minute of the old woman's rambling. But she droned on.

I wish she'd take a hint, the pastor thought. *Poor old Mizzie—her mind's starting to go, and she still pedals that three-wheeled bicycle all over town, making a spectacle of herself.* Even the older members shook their heads about it.

Finally she surrendered the microphone. "We'll be sure to pray about that, Mizzie," the pastor said and then looked at the young couple. This time the skinny fellow made it all the way to his feet.

"I—I don't know anything about talkin' in church," he began shakily. "But my old lady—" He indicated the girl at his side. "I mean, my, uh, wife and I really need a place to stay tonight. We saw the lights and came in."

The pastor watched the young man speak, touched by his need. "We're glad you did," the pastor said, "and I'm sure we can find you a place to stay. By the way, what's your name?"

The young man looked away shyly. "I'm Joe," he said, "and this is Mary."

A startled murmur was heard. "Joseph and Mary?" the pastor asked incredulously.

"Yeah, I know how it sounds," the young man said, growing red faced. "But it's true, really."

The pastor couldn't hold back a chuckle of wonderment. "Indeed it is," he said and quoted Hebrews 13:2 again. Inspired, he thanked the young man and prayed fervently for the couple's needs, the families gathered there, and the war-weary world's longing for peace on earth.

There was no doubt about it—the choir sounded sweeter than ever that night. The ancient story from Luke was never better read nor more poignant. Even the atmosphere seemed rare, closer to heaven, with the young couple sitting there in the front. When the time had come for the benediction, Pastor Torgenson looked out on the Christmas Eve faces and spoke from his heart.

"Let there be room in our inn tonight," he said. "Let us reach out to the Lord of Christmas and to one another. We may be different; but because he came, we can be one."

Downstairs, where the church ladies had prepared punch, coffee, and cookies, the congregation streamed in for a bit of fellowship. The pastor and his wife brought cups of coffee to the young man and woman, only to discover that several parishioners had already done the same.

"We'd be happy to have you stay at our house tonight, Joe and Mary," volunteered a middle-aged couple.

"We were going to say the same thing," said two others. A group of high schoolers brought cookies and punch to the strangers. Pastor Torgenson, smiling broadly, hugged his wife.

Over in the corner by the coffee percolator, old Mizzie Everett sat alone, with both hands around a cup of punch.

Angels We Have Heard on High   157

She squinted at the sea of people, seeming confused by the noise.

Suddenly she put down her punch and looked at her watch. As if on schedule, she picked up her purse and made her way to the door along the crowd's edge. Nobody noticed her leave.

The night was cold. Setting her jaw determinedly, Mizzie struggled against her arthritis to mount her three-wheeled bicycle.

So frail, these mortal bodies, she thought, dumping her purse in the bike's basket. Her legs strained, pumping the pedals. Iced puddles cracked under her wheels all the way out of town.

The city-limits sign flashed past. Wheezing, she knew she could go no further. Finally she slowed and parked by the side of the road.

The highway was deserted. Only the stars and heaven watched as she climbed the sloping field by the road, her breath coming in hoarse gasps. A dog barked in the distance.

Christmas Eve, she thought, looking at the sky. Just like that first Christmas Eve, when she had sung with the others. Oh, but that had been easy compared with this assignment. This time she'd had to take on a body for such a long time. Not like the Sodom and Gomorrah visit or the rest.

She stretched and felt a pain. It was good to be going home.

Smiling, she closed her eyes and reached heavenward. Slowly the creases in her face vanished, and the twisted hands unfurled. *Going home*, she thought.

Brighter and brighter her face glowed, her old coat transformed into a robe the color of the sun. It was an angel's robe.

At last, she thought, *at last*. There was a silent flash in the night, and Mizzie Everett was gone.

Joan 'n' the Whale

Angels We Have Heard on High